SCHOLASTIC

Tim Rasinski Presents...

Fabulously Famous Books

For Building Fluency™

p. 10: Excerpt from WINGS by Christopher Myers. Copyright © 2000 by Christopher Myers. Reprinted by permission of Scholastic Inc. All rights reserved.

Copyright © 2008 by Scholastic Inc.

All rights reserved.   Published by Scholastic Inc.   Printed in the U.S.A.

ISBN-13: 978-0-545-07129-1
ISBN-10: 0-545-07129-1

SCHOLASTIC, FABULOUSLY FAMOUS BOOKS FOR BUILDING FLUENCY, and associated logos and designs are trademarks and/or registered trademarks of Scholastic Inc.

1 2 3 4 5 6 7 8 9 10   40   16 15 14 13 12 11 10 09 08 07

Professional Guide

Written by Timothy Rasinski, Ph.D.

CONTENTS

Dear Educator,

Thank you for investing in the Tim Rasinski Presents *Fabulously Famous Books for Building Fluency*™ program. If you are a teacher who cherishes the richness of children's literature, wants to share the excitement of great literature with students, and wants to teach a critical but often neglected element of reading—fluency—in an engaging and authentic manner, then this library is for you.

Fluency is absolutely essential to the development of skilled and proficient reading. For many years, fluency was a neglected element of most reading programs. Now, although not neglected, it is often taught in mechanistic ways that focus students' attention away from what is most important in reading: meaning or comprehension.

My Fluency Library counters these mechanistic approaches by providing you and your students with some of the very best children's literature available. By itself, the library provides you with a superb collection of books that students will find engaging and satisfying. Even more important, however, while creating this library, I took special care to select books that lent themselves particularly well to fluency instruction and development.

All of the books included in the Fluency Library contain passages that have a strong sense of voice and can easily be performed orally for an audience. We know that guided repeated readings are particularly effective in developing fluency, but reading the same material over and over again can be tedious. Preparing for a performance requires students to practice or rehearse the text, but the excitement of preparing to perform before an audience turns the rehearsal into an engaging form of repeated reading. While rehearsing these texts that have a strong sense of voice, students create, or recreate, the voice of the author and the characters. They use their own voices to make the passages come alive—reading loudly, softly, quickly, and slowly, emphasizing words, pausing, phrasing, and employing other aspects of reading that some scholars call "prosody." I prefer to call it "reading with expression." We know that expressive, and not just fast, reading is a central part of fluency.

I invite you to use my library as a springboard for oral reading performances. Have students practice 50- to 200-word passage segments over the course of a week. Then on Fridays have them perform these or other passages at a special event designed to showcase their oral reading talents. Call your weekly gatherings whatever you like—poetry slam, classroom hootenanny, a reading idol, a karaoke club, or a literary reading. I guarantee that students will become more fluent readers. They will also become more confident readers who love language, who may choose to write in the style that they have performed, and who have a wonderful time with their teacher and classmates celebrating the joy of reading.

One particular outgrowth of the development of my library is worth mentioning. As I looked for material with voice and performance potential, I found myself drawn to a variety of literary genres. In my library you will not only find great stories and informational books, but you will also find books of poetry and rhymes, songs, stories written in the form of letters and diaries, famous speeches, and other texts that are often neglected in today's classrooms. The *Fabulously Famous Books for Building Fluency* library then provides you with a classroom set of materials that breaks the boundaries of traditional reading instruction. With these materials you will have an exceptional tool for introducing students to the wonderful richness of the literary world we live in.

Best wishes and please enjoy.

Authentic Reading Fluency Instruction: Bridging the Gap from Phonics to Comprehension

There has long been universal agreement that phonics, or word decoding, and reading comprehension are essential components of proficient reading and must be equally essential components of effective reading instruction. If reading is to be successful, readers must be able to turn the printed symbols on the page into their oral representations and, just as important, be able to understand the text that is represented by those printed symbols.

Only during the past decade, however, has reading fluency achieved similar prominence among the essential components of reading and reading instruction (National Reading Panel, 2000). Phonics and comprehension, although both essential to reading, are very different in both purpose and nature. I view reading fluency as the critical link between the two.

Defining Reading Fluency

Fluency refers to the ability to read the printed word (phonics) so effortlessly or automatically that readers can use their limited cognitive resources for the important task of making meaning (comprehension). It also involves reading the printed words (phonics) in ways that add to meaning (comprehension) through expression, phrasing, emphasis, pausing, and other features that linguists call *prosody*.

Fluency is made up of two components that bind phonics and comprehension: automaticity and prosody. Automaticity refers to the ability to read or decode words effortlessly. The theory of automaticity in reading (LaBerge & Samuels, 1974) suggests that all readers have a limited amount of attention or cognitive resources that they can devote to reading. Any of these resources that are applied to word decoding cannot be used for comprehension. Thus, readers who spend too much mental effort on word decoding often do not comprehend well what they read.

The goal of proficient reading is not just accurate decoding of words but automatic decoding. Automaticity in word decoding is achieved through guided practice, in very much the same way as driving a car, hitting a golf ball, or any other activity for which automaticity can be acquired. Automaticity is normally measured by reading rate or speed. Fast reading generally is indicative of automatic word decoding; slower, more laborious reading is suggestive of word reading that is not automatic and that requires more cognitive attention on the part of the reader.

When word decoding is automatic, readers have cognitive resources available to make meaning. One way that readers make or add to meaning is by manipulating their voices. Prosody involves the oral language features that usually fall under the general category of expression. More precisely, however, prosody can involve tone, volume, pacing, phrasing, pausing, emphasis, and dialect. When readers read with appropriate prosody, they are giving evidence that they are making meaning while they read. When appropriate prosody is not present, it is likely that readers are not attending sufficiently to meaning.

Prosody is best achieved through guided practice in which readers explore how meaning is made or reflected through the voice while reading aloud. It is most easily measured by simply listening to readers read orally and making a judgment as to the extent to which the oral reading sounds like real language, as opposed to language that may sound artificial or mechanical. Teachers often use descriptive rubrics to guide their judgments of prosodic or expressive oral reading.

How Important Is Reading Fluency?

Research over the past decade has shown that appropriate instruction in reading fluency does indeed lead to significant gains in reading (see Chard, Vaughn, & Taylor, 2002; Kuhn & Stahl, 2000; Rasinski & Hoffman, 2003). Moreover, these gains in reading were found in students at various grade levels, among both struggling and proficient students, and when instruction was done outside of the classroom as well as in school. In some cases, the gains noted in reading comprehension and achievement were remarkable. For example, students made two to three years of progress for every one year of instruction in reading fluency (Griffith & Rasinski, 2004).

It has become well recognized over the past decade that reading fluency is an issue that needs to be addressed instructionally if all students are to achieve it. Fluency and phonics are particularly important for readers who struggle. Duke, Pressley, and Hilden (2004), for example, argue that upwards of 75% or more of students who manifest significant difficulties in reading comprehension and overall reading achievement have phonics and fluency issues that are major hindrances to their progress in reading comprehension. Thus, for struggling readers in particular, reading fluency must be an instructional priority.

Teaching Reading Fluency Comprehensively, Effectively, Appropriately, and Authentically

An instructional design that includes teacher modeling of fluency, teacher guidance of, and assistance to students while they read, plenty of practice and/or repeated readings of a passage, and explorations of meaning and words within the passage is the ideal and integrated approach for effective fluency instruction. A routine that is highly effective in teaching fluency includes the following steps.

Modeling. The teacher should read the passage with appropriate speed and expression and then discuss how he or she read the passage with the students so that students can develop their own sense of what makes for fluent reading.

Reading aloud together. This allows the students to support one another and receive support from the teacher. Group readings can be done in a variety of ways, including the entire class, small groups, individuals reading certain parts, or echo choral reading. Responsibility for reading the passage gradually shifts from the teacher to the students.

Practicing. Individuals, pairs, or small groups of students are asked to practice reading the passage orally on their own. The teacher is still involved in listening, giving feedback and encouragement, coaching, and monitoring students' participation and level of fluency.

Performing. Students perform their practiced passages for an audience. At this point, teachers might arrange a poetry slam, a hootenanny and sing-along, a reader's theater festival, a "reading idol" competition, or some other special event to showcase students' oral reading talents.

Word study. Once a text is memorized, students are less likely to continue examining the passage visually. So it's a good idea to have students choose five to ten words from the practiced text to place on a word wall or in journals or word banks for display and study. The words are then practiced in isolation, grouped or sorted, to force students to look closely at the words. The growing body of words can also be used for word games and for other word study activities at various times during the school day.

Additional practice. The best place for additional practice is at home. This additional practice before a different audience will continue to build students' fluency and confidence in their reading ability.

This is a generic lesson sequence that can be covered in 20 minutes or less. It can be a weekly routine with Fridays reserved for student performances, or it can be implemented in some other way that may require two to three days to complete one lesson.

The key to the lessons and to students' development in reading fluency is the gradual release of responsibility from teacher to student, and it is focused on oral interpretation of the text—making meaning with words and voice. Students who practice in this way will not only show improvement in reading the texts they practice, but, more importantly, it will demonstrate their improvements in fluency and comprehension when reading other authentic reading passages not previously encountered.

Three Libraries, One Focus

The Tim Rasinski Presents *Fabulously Famous Books for Building Fluency*™ program includes the following materials:

▶ This Professional Guide, which provides you with information on how to use *Fabulously Famous Books for Building Fluency* to develop effective fluency instruction using authentic children's literature.

▶ A set of 32, two-page lessons, one for each book in the Fluency Library. Each lesson presents a featured passage from the text and instructions on using the passage to teach vocabulary and model fluent reading. The cards also provide ideas for repeated reading practice in the classroom and for writing and oral performance activities.

▶ My *Three-Minute Reading Assessment* book, which allows you to gather baseline data on your students' reading development and then chart their progress over the school year.

▶ Word Ladder activities that provide you with an engaging and effective method for teaching spelling, word recognition, and vocabulary.

▶ A Teacher Resources CD-ROM, on which you will find printable files for the blackline masters and the lessons.

▶ The Fluency Library. This main component of the *Fabulously Famous Books for Building Fluency* program is the set of books (at three levels, A, B, and C) that you and your students will enjoy throughout the year.

Library A   **Library B**   **Library C**

Teacher Resources CD-ROM

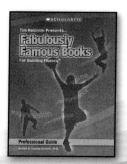

Professional Guide

Sample Lesson

Provides summary of fluency skills, practice strategies, and vocabulary words featured in the lesson.

You may want to read the entire book to students (or have them read it on their own) so that readers get a sense of the whole story.

Featured Passage from each book selected to highlight particular fluency skills.

■SCHOLASTIC

Tim Rasinski Presents...

Fabulously Famous Books

For Building Fluency

Lesson Objectives:

Modeled Reading: Punctuation Clues (Exclamation Marks)

Individualized Practice: Cooperative Repeated Reading; Echo Reading/Buddy Reading

Fluency Performance: Scripts (Writing); Reader's Theater (Oral Presentation)

Key Vocabulary: exploded, dropped. sailed

Modeled Reading

Before Reading

You may want to begin by writing the Featured Passage on the board or on chart paper.

Discuss the concept of friendship. Ask: *What makes someone a friend? How should friends treat one another? Have you ever become friends with someone you didn't expect to like at first?* Explain that in this book, the narrator makes friends with an unusual boy.

Talk about key vocabulary words. Pronounce the words and have students say each word two or three times. Provide student-friendly definitions of the words and use the words in sentences where possible. Ask students to choose two or three words to add to the classroom word wall and to individual word banks.

Featured Passage From:

Wings

by Christopher Myers
pages 37–42

When the neighborhood kids saw
the policeman yelling at him, they **exploded**
with laughter.
Ikarus **dropped** to the ground.
"Stop!" I cried. "Leave him alone."
And they did.

I called to Ikarus
and he **sailed** closer to me.
I told him
what someone should have long ago:
"Your flying is beautiful."

For the first time, I saw Ikarus smile.
At that moment I forgot
about the kids who had laughed
at him and me. I was just glad that
Ikarus had found his wings again.

Wings

Before Reading activities build background and initiate classroom discussion about important themes from the story.

Vocabulary words (Tier 2, related, or high-frequency) important to understanding the passage and key for word study are featured.

Fluency skills are modeled aloud by the teacher. Students are engaged in discussion about the fluency skill being taught, and participate in a choral reading of the passage with the teacher.

During Reading

- Read the book aloud. Ask students to listen for how the narrator and Ikarus become friends.

- Repeat pages 37–42 two more times. Place emphasis on the exclamations in the lines, *"Stop!" I cried.* and *"Look at that amazing boy!"*

- Explain to students that an exclamation mark tells the reader about something exciting or surprising. When the narrator's or character's words end with an exclamation mark, she is passionate, or has strong feelings about what she's saying.

- Read the passage a second time with a robotic, unexpressive tone of voice. Solicit from students the difference between the two readings. Ask: *Which reading was easier to understand? Why?*

- Read the passage chorally with students several times, as time permits.

Individualized Practice

Repeated Reading: Cooperative Repeated Reading

- Organize students into pairs.

- Each student should practice reading the passage at least three times. Partners should listen, provide assistance if needed, and give feedback. As they read, students should pay particular attention to punctuation clues and to how these clues affect their expression.

- Students may also fill out the Cooperative Repeated Reading Response Form from the Teacher Resources CD-ROM.

Echo Reading/Buddy Reading

- For students who are struggling with punctuation clues, conduct individual Echo Reading practice with them.

- Read one phrase of the Featured Passage and have the student Echo Read the phrase back.

- While you do Echo Reading with struggling students, other students may do Buddy Reading using *Wings*. Pairs of students can decide whether to alternate reading each page of the book, reading the book chorally, or repeating the Featured Passage chorally.

Fluency Performance

Scripts (Writing)

- Have students work in groups of five to create a Reader's Theater script for the Featured Passage. The different parts could be the narrator, Ikarus, the policeman, and the jeering kids. Model script adaptation as necessary.

- Then encourage student groups to choose their own passages from *Wings* for adaptation.

Reader's Theater (Oral Presentation)

- Provide students time to practice their scripts. Ask students to take copies home with them. They should read the script for family members and friends as many times as possible.

- On subsequent days, groups can quickly practice and then perform their scripts for the class.

In-class writing activities encourage students to demonstrate and apply the fluency skills learned and featured in the lesson.

Additional activities provide fluency practice for the whole class and for struggling students.

Fun and engaging opportunities invite and challenge students to present their written materials to the class using various oral presentation forms.

Wings

SCHOLASTIC

Page 2 of 2

TM & © Scholastic Inc. All rights reserved.

11

Implementing *Fabulously Famous Books for Building Fluency*

Regardless of the type of classroom you teach in, *Fabulously Famous Books for Building Fluency* can help you make fluency instruction an integral part of your regular reading instruction.

Literature-Based Classrooms

If your reading curriculum is literature based, my library is a natural choice for you. You and your students can use the books in the library as the foundation for your group or core reading activities. In addition to the regular discussions and strategy activities that are part of the classroom experience, students can select passages from the book to practice and perform. These performances can be wonderful culminating experiences for each book study.

Basal Classrooms

If your reading curriculum is organized around a basal or core reading program, *Fabulously Famous Books for Building Fluency* can be a perfect complement. Students can choose books from the library for their independent reading and follow up their reading with oral performances of memorable passages from the chosen books.

You can also use the library to supplement any fluency instruction found in your core program. For many struggling readers, lack of fluency is at the heart of their reading problems. Additional instruction using my Fluency Library along with the detailed fluency lesson plans for each book can help many students overcome fluency and comprehension problems.

Intervention Settings

If you happen to be an interventionist, reading specialist, Title I teacher or tutor, special education teacher, or any one of the many other titles that refer to a teacher who works with students experiencing significant difficulties in reading, *Fabulously Famous Books for Building Fluency* can serve as your main intervention program or as a key complement to your existing intervention program.

Research suggests that fluency problems are the root cause of students' reading difficulties. Overcoming the fluency problem may help these students make significant strides in their reading achievement. As a main intervention program, I suggest using the detailed lessons included in this program to teach fluency. The lessons also have additional suggestions and activities for helping students learn word decoding and vocabulary. Since the books are authentic texts that students love, they naturally foster discussion and lead to other activities that promote reading comprehension.

As an adjunct to an existing intervention program, the books and fluency lessons provide a welcome counterpoint and relief from the direct instruction that is found in so many intervention programs. Moreover, this program will provide additional support and instruction for overcoming fluency problems that may be the source of students' general reading difficulties.

Home Involvement

Fabulously Famous Books for Building Fluency is ideal for use as an outreach program into your students' homes. Among the easiest things parents can do to help their children become better readers is to read to them, read with them, and listen to their children read aloud. Since fluency is fostered by all three activities, involving parents in reading selected passages from the books in the Fluency Library to and with their children, and then later coaching their children to practice reading the passages with expression, will no doubt build children's fluency and confidence in their reading. Best of all, reading is a wonderful way for parents and children to spend time together.

How to Read Aloud

One of the best activities that can be done with a book or a featured passage in the classroom is to read it aloud to your students. One of the fondest memories of school that most adults have is being read to by a teacher. Not only is reading aloud a wonderful way to build enthusiasm and motivation for reading, the research suggests that students who are read to on a regular basis tend to have larger vocabularies and are better able to comprehend text than students who are not read to by their teachers.

In addition to these benefits, reading aloud fits naturally into any program designed to teach reading fluency. When a teacher reads to her students, she is able to model what she means by fluency. Through her phrasing, emphasis, rate, and intonation, the teacher can demonstrate to students how she has added to the reading experience through her oral interpretation of the text.

Conversely, some of the best teachers I know will occasionally slip into disfluent reading—reading in a monotone, without phrasing, expression, or enthusiasm, and at a very slow or very fast rate. Students soon find that listening to such a reading is not enjoyable and even makes the reading hard to understand. The lesson learned here is that when students read, they need to read with appropriate expression and enthusiasm, not only to help themselves but to help anyone who may be listening to them.

Find 10–20 minutes each day to read to your students; make it a regular feature of the school day. Choose the very best materials that will leave your students begging for more each time you have to end the read-aloud session. If some of those great books come from my Fluency Library, you'll find that they lend themselves very well to reading with appropriate expression.

Before you read to students, be sure to look over the passage you are going to read and practice it. Both children and adults need to rehearse in order to read fluently. Make note of the difficult words and identify in advance any parts of the text where you might want to emphasize words, change your reading pace, or create long, dramatic pauses. Think about the questions you might ask students after the reading and what you might want to draw their attention to during the post-reading discussion. Talking about how your reading was fluent, and why, should be an important part of the post-reading discussion.

While reading, have younger students sit near you on the floor. Older students can sit at their desks. Encourage them to listen to how you interpret the text orally, to listen for interesting words that might go on the word wall, and to try to make sense of the passage as it is read. You may have to read a poem or other short poetic text several times before students can fully understand and internalize the text.

At the end of the oral reading, discuss what you did to make the words come alive through your reading. Explore with students how meaning might change if different words were emphasized or read in slightly different way. If you use a classroom fluency rubric, have students rate your reading and use the rating as a springboard for discussion. Ask students what interesting words they heard during your read-aloud. Write the words on a classroom word wall and discuss them. Encourage students to use the words in their own oral and written language. As a class, discuss any nuances to the meanings of the words, and teach any phonics elements related to the words.

How to Do an Oral Recitation Lesson and Story Map

After studying the role of oral reading in traditional reading instruction since the 1800s, as well as scholarly literature on the impact of oral reading on struggling readers, James Hoffman (1987; Hoffman & Crone, 1985) developed the Oral Recitation Lesson (ORL), an instructional procedure involving modeling, support and coaching, repeated reading, and performance. Easily implemented in a regular classroom where basal stories and informational passages are part of the reading program, ORL is particularly effective with low-achieving readers. The lesson is made up of two basic components: direct instruction and indirect instruction. Each component contains several steps. (See page 19 for guidelines.)

The direct instruction component begins with the teacher reading a story to the instructional group of several students. When she's finished, she and her students engage in a discussion of the text and, on the board or on chart paper, create a story map together that includes the story's basic elements. (See sample below and on your Teacher Resources CD-ROM.) The teacher writes the students' responses verbatim, as in a language experience activity. The completed story map is used as a visual aid to construct a written summary of the story. Third grade teacher Jean Larson says that this helps her students get a good overall sense of the story. (See completed sample, page 17.)

TRCD BLM #05

Tim Rasinski Presents...

Fabulously Famous Books

For Building Fluency

Name Giovanni Ameri

Date 05/12/07

Story Map

Title of Story I Lost My Tooth In Africa

Setting—Place Mali, West Africa

Setting—Time Today, 2007

Main Characters Amina, her mom and dad, N'na, her uncle and aunt.

Problem Amina looses her tooth in Africa.

Events

On the plane to Mali, Amina realizes she has a wiggly tooth.

The next day she looses her tooth when she brushes her teeth.

She and her dad put it under a calabash and wait for the African tooth fairy to bring her a chicken.

Amina gets a rooster and a hen.

Resolution Right before Amina leaves to back to America the baby chick she got

from the African tooth fairy hatches and her uncle tells her he will take care of them.

Amina can't wait to come back to Africa and take care of all of her chickens.

Sample Completed Story Map

Hoffman (1987) describes the second step in the direct instruction component as fast-paced and interactive. Jean begins with a mini-lesson on the importance of effective oral expression, focusing on aspects such as pitch, stress, and juncture. Then, with appropriate enthusiasm and expression, she reads a text segment from the story that students will be expected to read. The segment increases in length from a few sentences to an entire page or more as students become increasingly fluent in their reading. Students then practice reading the segment, individually and/or chorally, with Jean listening in and providing support and feedback to improve oral expression.

For the third step of the direct instruction component, Jean has her students select a passage from a text, usually about one page long, that they wish to perform. The students practice independently and then perform for the group. After each performance, Jean showers her students with useful comments such as, "Wow! You had great volume. We could all hear you well!" or "The expression you used helped me understand what the author was trying to say. Great job!" The direct instruction component may require two to four reading-group sessions to complete. When the work on one story is complete, focus instruction on another story that is as challenging as or is slightly more challenging than the one just completed.

The indirect instruction component is a whole-class activity that takes approximately 10 minutes. Students work with stories that were assigned earlier in the direct instruction component. They practice reading their assigned story using mumble reading (soft, barely audible oral reading) so that all students can practice without disturbing one another. During this time, Jean works with individual students, checking for mastery. Mastery for the second grade, according to Hoffman, is a minimum of 98% word recognition accuracy and 75 words-per-minute fluency, with good expression. Once Jean signs off a student on one story, she guides him to another story that is as difficult as or more challenging than the one just completed.

Hoffman (1987) reported that second-grade students who used the ORL made progress in reading, especially in cases where little progress had been made previously. Students progressed from simple word identification to comprehension. Other research (Reutzel & Hollingsworth, 1993; Reutzel, Hollingsworth, & Eldredge, 1994) has found that students who received ORL made gains in both reading fluency and comprehension.

Teaching an Oral Recitation Lesson

The ORL is meant to be used in regular classroom settings, particularly with students who are experiencing difficulty in reading. Authentic narrative and informational passages from basal readers or trade books may be used.

Direct Instruction Component (2–4 days per story, 30–45 minutes per day, done in small groups)

Part 1: Read the story aloud to students. After the reading, work with students to construct a story map that contains major elements such as setting (time and place), characters, problem, and resolution to the problem. Act as a scribe and write the students' responses verbatim on a chart or chalkboard.

Using the story map as a guide, write a story summary that is brief, accurate, and complete.

Select a memorable portion of the story (from a few sentences to an entire page or more) for the next part of the lesson.

Part 2: Provide a mini-lesson on the elements of good, expressive, and meaningful reading. Model fluent oral reading of the memorable portion of the story that you selected. Have students practice reading the selected portion alone, in pairs, and/or chorally. Coach them by giving feedback, support, and praise.

Part 3: Have students select a portion of the text for performance. Give them plenty of opportunity for practice, and when they're ready, have them perform the texts for their classmates. Be sure to offer positive feedback after every performance.

Indirect Instruction Component (daily for approximately 10 minutes; done by the entire class)

Assign or ask students to choose a story, or a portion of a story, that has been covered in the direct instruction component. Have students practice their story using mumble reading so that all students can practice without disturbing one another. As they practice, check to see if students have achieved mastery in word recognition (98% word recognition accuracy) and fluency (75 words-per-minute, with good expression).

Assign the next story or passage and repeat the process with students who achieve mastery.

How to Do a Fluency Development Lesson

In 1998, my colleague Nancy Padak and I (Rasinski & Padak, 1998) examined the reading behavior of elementary school students who were recommended by their classroom teacher to receive Title I instruction. We looked at various aspects of their reading, including decoding, fluency, and comprehension. Students in every grade, on average, performed below grade-level expectations in all three areas. One finding, however, surprised us: The area in which students performed the lowest by far was reading fluency. Students read the connected text we gave them in such a slow, disjointed, and labored manner that we wondered how they could possibly understand any of it. We surmised that reading fluency is key to reading proficiency and that lack of fluency is a significant contributor to students' difficulties in reading. Our conclusion was later confirmed by the findings of the National Reading Panel.

In response to the findings of our study, Padak and I developed a synergistic lesson for teaching reading fluency called the Fluency Development Lesson (FDL) (Rasinski & Padak, 2001), which is outlined on page 23.

FDL begins with the teacher reading aloud several times (modeling/repeated reading) a short, usually predictable, text such as a poem or a passage from a basal story. Second grade teacher Harry Parker, for example, uses his booming voice to draw his students into the daily poems that he uses in his fluency development lessons. Then he repeats the poem in a variety of other voices, including a staccato, unexpressive robot-like voice, which his students dislike, to illustrate disfluent reading. Harry then spends a few minutes talking with his students about the meaning of the poem and discussing any difficult or unusual words.

Next, Harry and his students read the poem chorally several times, in various ways (oral support reading). Harry then pairs up his students. Each student reads the poem to his or her partner three times (repeated reading). The partner listens, provides help when necessary, and encourages the reader. After the third reading, the students reverse roles, and the listener becomes the reader. Harry feels it is important to encourage the listeners to be supportive and to give helpful feedback.

After this practice time, Harry calls the students together and offers them the opportunity to perform for an audience. The audience is usually the class itself, but sometimes Harry sends students off to perform for other classes; the school principal, secretary, and janitor; parent volunteers; and teachers who aren't on duty (more repeated reading).

After the performances, Harry and his students choose two or three interesting words from the text and add them to their individual word banks and the classroom word wall. Later, these words are used for word practice, sorts, games, and other activities.

Harry extends FDL by making two copies of the poem for each student. The students keep one copy in their poetry folders so they can reread and enjoy it later. The other copy goes home. Each day, as homework, students must find as many people as possible to listen to them read their FDL poem (more repeated reading). Parents, grandparents, brothers, sisters, relatives, and neighbors listen to the student read his or her poem or passage one or more times. Harry primes parents about this early in the school year. He not only tells them that their students will be reading a poem or passage each day to develop fluency, but he also talks to them about the importance of repeated reading and encouragement. After each reading, the listener signs the back of the poem and adds a word or two of praise, which automatically enrolls them in the "Lucky Listener Club." This activity has evolved into a friendly competition to see who can come to class each morning with the greatest number of signatures. This is not only fun for the students, but it also tells Harry which students are doing the most repeated readings. Harry and his students usually read the poem a couple more times chorally before moving on to the new poem for the day.

FDL is fast paced. Harry's entire lesson, for example, takes less than 15 minutes to complete. Once students get the hang of the routine, it doesn't need to be explained. So instead of listening to directions, Harry's students are reading—and they read a lot! Moreover, for students who are still struggling with fluency, this form of modeled, supported reading is just what they need to help them improve.

In 1992, three colleagues and I worked with second-grade teachers in urban schools, implementing FDL from October to May (Rasinski, Padak, Linek, & Sturtevant, 1994). We found that students made substantial gains in their reading fluency, as well as in their overall reading, as measured by an informal reading inventory. Indeed, their gains were greater than those of a similar group of students who spent the same amount of time in reading instruction, with the same texts, but engaged in other forms of instruction. Moreover, we found that students and teachers enjoyed FDL. One student, Joey, told us, "I like it because when we are done, I can read my poem really good." Students became successful at reading FDL texts—and that success continued as the students read new, unfamiliar texts.

But perhaps the greatest evidence of FDL's effectiveness lies in its staying power. Teachers continue to practice FDL even now, years after the completion of the study. And we can see why: We have used a version of FDL in our university reading clinic for years and have found it to work well with students of all ages who have difficulty with reading fluency.

Teaching a Fluency Development Lesson

Try to do the FDL on a regular basis, daily if possible. Use short passages of about 100–200 words. Highly predictable poems work well, as do consecutive segments of a short story read over several days.

▶ Make two copies of the FDL passage for each student. Write the text on chart paper or on the board for choral reading.

▶ Read the text aloud several times and in different voices while students listen or follow along silently.

▶ Discuss the meaning of the text, as well as your reading of the text, with students.

▶ Read the text with the class several times, in variations of choral reading.

▶ Pair up students and have them read the text to each other, three times each, with the listener offering support and encouragement.

▶ Have students reassemble and perform their texts for an audience: their classmates, other classrooms, the school staff, and parents.

▶ Ask students to choose two or three words from the text for the classroom word wall and individual word banks. Study the words later using word sorts, games, and practice.

▶ Have students put one copy of the text in their poetry folders for later reading at school. Have them take the other copy home to read to family, friends, and neighbors. The listeners should offer praise and support and sign the back of the student's text.

▶ Begin the next day with students reading the text from the previous day chorally and individually. Then begin the routine again with a new text.

How to Use Choral Reading

Choral reading, where groups of students read the same text aloud, is one of the most common forms of reading in the primary grades—and it is gaining popularity in middle schools. Why? It is a great way to maximize the amount of reading done per student. (20 students reading a 20-line page of text in unison certainly results in more reading per student than one student reading one line of the text one at a time.)

Choral reading is also a wonderful way to build community in the classroom. For example, each morning as students read and recite the Pledge of Allegiance, they are declaring their unity as a community of learners. This routine also provides support for those students who are not yet fluent readers.

Choral reading also builds fluency. As students read a text together orally, they are supporting one another. Those students who may not be good readers are supported by the more fluent oral readings of their classmates. If students read a text chorally together a few times, even the struggling readers will be able to read it on their own with good fluency. More importantly, when students move on to other passages, some of what they have learned through their choral reading will carry over to the new reading.

In Carol Tesh's third grade class, students read chorally at least one new poem each day, as well as several familiar poems. Carol writes the poems on chart paper so all the students can see the text, and she has the students read them at various times during the day—at the opening of the school day, before morning recess, at transition times, after lunch, and before the end of the day. According to Carol, "Coming together to read in unison throughout the day reinforces the fact that we are a team and we need to work together, whether it's in reading, in writing, on the playground, or wherever."

Carol has noticed that during these choral readings, even the worst strugglers can read. "They seem to get the cue from the other readers in the class. We'll read a poem once, twice, three times a day or even more. And each time we read, their voices get stronger and more confident. Even the students who have the most difficult time in reading can read by the third time through. After listening to their classmates read and then reading *while* listening to their classmates read, many struggling students come up to me near the end of the day and read the poem out loud on their own." Clearly, these students are benefiting from the support of both Carol and their classmates.

Types of Choral Reading

Normally during choral reading, the entire group reads one text completely and in unison, but there are alternatives (Vacca, Vacca, & Gove, 2000).

Refrain. In refrain choral reading, one student reads most of the text, with the whole group chiming in to read key segments chorally. The song read by the mother in Robert Munsch's *Love You Forever* is a fine example of refrain. The first and last stanza of Robert Service's poem *The Cremation of Sam McGee* is a good choice as well. Copy text such as these on the board and read them as a class.

Line-a-Child. In line-a-child choral reading, each student reads one or two lines of a text, usually a rhyme or a poem, individually, and then the whole group reads the final line or lines together. The rhyme "One Two Buckle My Shoe" and the poem "Good Books, Good Times" are perfect for line-a-child.

Dialogue. Dialogue is similar to reader's theater (see page 42 for more information). Texts that work best for this form of choral reading contain different speaking parts, such as the dog and cat from Donald Hall's *I Am the Dog, I Am the Cat,* or the narrator and the cat from the poem "Pussy Cat, Pussy Cat":

Narrator:	Pussy cat, pussy cat, where have you been?
Cat:	I've been to London to see the Queen.
Narrator:	Pussy cat, pussy cat, what did you do there?
Cat:	I frightened a little mouse under the chair.

One student or a section of the class would read the part of the narrator, while another individual or group reads the part of the cat.

Antiphonal Reading. For this version, divide the whole class into groups (e.g., boys and girls; rows 1, 2, and 3) and assign sections of a passage to each subgroup. Then, when reading the text, each section is read by one of the subgroups. If the passage contains a refrain, the entire class should read it together. A variation of antiphonal reading is to have individuals act as groups. Individuals read certain sections, and whole groups read other sections.

Call-and-Response. One student reads a line or two of a text, and the rest of the class responds by repeating the lines or reading the next few lines or the refrain. Song lyrics and historical documents such as the Declaration of Independence are good choices for call-and-response reading.

Cumulative Choral Reading. An individual or a small group reads one line or section of a passage. Another reader chimes in for the next line, and a few more readers for the lines that follow. By the time the end of the text is reached, the entire class should be reading. Certain texts, such as the Preamble to the Constitution of the United States, are well suited to a cumulative choral reading. The reading begins with one or two students reading, "We the people . . ." By the end of the Preamble, the entire class reads, ". . . do ordain and establish this constitution for the United States of America." This layering of voices can be inspiring because it brings the notion of "we the people" to life.

Cumulative choral reading can work in the other direction as well, with the whole class reading at first and then, with each succeeding line, one or more voices dropping out. By the end of the text, only one or two students should be reading.

Choral Singing. Another form of choral reading is choral singing, which offers the same benefits as the preceding variations, plus some. The melody of a song makes its lyrics easy to memorize. Have you ever gotten a song stuck in your head and found yourself singing or saying its lyrics for the rest of the day? That's the power of melody and well-written, predictable lyrics.

Choral singing is an excellent way to introduce beginning readers to written text. Once students have memorized the lyrics, you can read them as a text, separate from the melody. From there, you can break down the lyrics into individual lines and finally into words. Words can be broken down into letters and patterns for building decoding skills. The goal in decoding is to get students to a point where they can recognize the words without the support of the melody or other contextual elements of the text.

Impromptu Choral Reading. Finally, imagine a group of readers standing in front of an audience reading a poem aloud. The reading begins in a standard way with one student reading a line, but then it moves in an unpredictable direction. One student reads some lines, and other lines are read by groups of two, three, or more students. All students read some lines. At various points in the reading, some students emphasize particular words. This is impromptu choral reading, and although it may seem chaotic, it can make for an impressive and compelling performance.

Essentially, in impromptu choral reading, each reader chooses whatever line, word, or phrase he or she would like to read. In my experience, students tend to choose lines that have a strong emotional impact or contain content that is essential to understanding the piece. During the performance, some lines are read by individuals and others by groups of varying sizes. And if nobody chooses a passage, which rarely happens, at least one reader always jumps in to save the performance. Impromptu choral reading is empowering for students, and it adds even greater variety to the list of choral reading possibilities.

Before attempting these forms of choral reading, allow time for planning and practice. Be sure to look over the text or passage and ask yourself what form of choral reading would work best. Then, be sure to practice the piece several times with your students before performing it for any audience. The practice itself is a wonderful way to build fluency and proficiency in reading. Almost any text can be read chorally, and my Fluency Library provides a wealth of material that can be used for choral reading. Poetry is a natural for choral reading. In addition to poems, look for shorter texts, including memorable segments from stories, letters and diary entries, short stories, song lyrics, and even reader's theater scripts, which can be read with groups of readers taking on individual roles. Anything that has a good rhythm and distinct parts can be adapted for choral reading. Also, texts that have community value, such as the Pledge of Allegiance, the Preamble to the Constitution, and patriotic songs, are excellent choices. Try to match the type of text you choose to one of the forms of choral reading listed above.

Choral reading has been around for a long time, but only recently have we discovered the power it has to nurture students' development in reading and reading fluency.

How to Use Paired Reading

During the late 1960s and early 1970s, an oral reading activity called the Neurological Impress method produced remarkable progress in special education students who used the method with a tutor for even short periods of time. The method involved two readers—a good reader (the tutor) and a struggling reader (the tutee)—who read orally together for 10–15 minutes. Both readers read the same text at the same time. The tutor sat slightly behind the tutee so that the tutor's voice was directed into one of the tutee's ears. Although the method showed great promise, it never received the widespread attention and application I think it deserved. Perhaps it was the name, Neurological Impress, which sounds more like a punishment or a freakish scientific experiment than a teaching method. Regardless of the reason, Neurological Impress was not a widely accepted practice.

During the 1980s, an English psychologist named Keith Topping made Neurological Impress more popular and accessible to users. First, he named his activity Paired Reading. Then he modified the nature of the activity itself. Rather than the tutor reading into the ear of another reader, the tutor and tutee simply sat side by side and read the same text aloud together. Topping was interested in developing simple ways in which parents could help their children with reading, and in paired reading he found a winner. Parents who did paired reading with their children for 10–20 minutes per day accelerated the progress of their children's overall reading achievement by a factor of three to five. So children who were previously making two weeks' progress in reading for every month's worth of instruction would begin to make six weeks' to ten weeks' progress for every month of instruction when parents began to do paired reading with them!

Something special happens when children read and are supported by a parent or another reader who reads with them. The children begin to match words produced orally with words in print, and their sight vocabulary and word recognition skills begin to develop. They also begin to read with fluency, matching the expression and rate of their reading partner.

The beauty of paired reading is its simplicity. Paired reading is an activity shared by two readers, one stronger than the other (parent–child, teacher–student, older student–younger student, or two same-age students). It works best with students who are experiencing difficulty with decoding and general fluency.

Try to make paired reading a daily activity in your classroom for at least six consecutive weeks, with each session lasting from 10–20 minutes. Start by having the student choose the reading material. It might be something she's reading for pleasure or reading as a class assignment. A book from my Fluency Library would be a perfect choice. As with any direct-teaching activity, the greatest gain will occur when the difficulty of the material is at the student's instructional level (i.e., 90–95% accuracy in word recognition)—neither too hard nor too easy.

Sit side by side in comfortable chairs that allow for good posture. Read together in a natural, comfortable manner, looking directly at the text as one person (usually the student) follows along with a finger. Adjust your reading rate to match or gently "push" the student. You will also need to adjust your voice to match the demands of the text. For example, if a portion of the text seems a bit difficult for the student, read in a somewhat louder voice and give the student more forceful verbal cues. When the student is reading successfully, tone down your voice so that it provides just the right level of support.

If the student makes a decoding error during the reading, simply state the correct pronunciation of the word while pointing at it, ask the student to do the same, and then move on. Paired reading is *not* the time to stop and begin a decoding lesson, which would only interrupt fluency and meaning. Rather, you may wish to make a mental note of the miscued words and chat with the student about them after the session—how the words are pronounced, what cues in the words help us with pronunciation, what the words mean, and so forth.

When the student feels confident reading the text on her own, she should give you a prearranged "solo" signal, such as a gentle elbow nudge to the side, which gives her control over the experience. At this point you should stop reading aloud but continue to read silently and monitor the student's reading. If the student runs into trouble, immediately resume reading orally. The student may also signal you to resume oral reading without experiencing difficulty.

If the student needs a brief break, you can read orally while she continues to read silently or in a whisper. Before the reading, be sure to give the student a signal for letting you know that she wants to proceed this way. (A finger tap on the page can work just fine.)

It's a good idea to keep track of paired reading sessions, whether they occur in the classroom or at home between parent and child. Try to do paired reading at least five times per week, 10–20 minutes per session, for at least six consecutive weeks. When paired reading is done regularly in this way, students are more likely to make greater progress because the progress from one day carries over to the next, and the success snowballs.

Although intended originally as a parent involvement activity, the child's paired reading partner can be anyone who is willing to play the role—teacher, teacher aide, parent volunteer in the school or classroom, older students, or even a classmate (buddy reading) who may be a slightly better reader than the tutee. The key is to read together so that the student reinforces his vision of the text and words with his voice and the voice of the partner. (See the Paired Reading Record and Response sheets on your TRCD in the BLM folder, BLM #s 01 and 02.)

Teaching Paired Reading

▶ Allow the student to choose the material to read; pleasure reading or school assignments are both acceptable.

▶ Find a comfortable, quiet place to sit side by side. Position the text so that it can be easily viewed by both of you.

▶ If the text is a continuation of a previous day's reading, quickly review what was read earlier. Review with the student the procedures for doing paired reading and what the student may need to be aware of in reading the upcoming text.

▶ Begin reading together. Adjust your intonation and rate to the student's level of proficiency. Read with a distinct and expressive voice that is slightly faster than the student would normally read on his own.

▶ Have the student follow the text with a finger as you both read.

▶ If the student makes an error (or hesitates for a few seconds on a word), wait to see if he corrects it. If he doesn't, pronounce the word and have the student repeat it. Then continue reading. Review and discuss errors at the end of the session.

▶ Decide on a nonverbal "solo" signal with the student (e.g., a gentle elbow nudge to your side) that he can use to tell you that he wants to read independently. When such a signal is given, you should either stop reading aloud or read in a whisper that "shadows" the student's reading.

  If the student encounters difficulty during "solo" reading, provide help and resume reading aloud. If the student wishes to read independently again later, he should use the "solo" signal

▶ At the end of the session, chat with the student about the reading behaviors that are improving. Praise his efforts. Talk about any particularly difficult words or portions of the text. Discuss the meaning of the text.

▶ Complete the paired reading Record and Response Sheet. (See TRCD BLM #s 01 and 02.)

How to Use Buddy Reading

Fourth-grade teacher Lorraine was concerned that many of her students were not actually reading during Sustained Silent Reading (SSR) time but instead were browsing through books they selected, chatting with friends, and so forth. Recognizing that reading is largely a social activity, Lorraine replaced SSR with a buddy reading program.

During buddy reading, students at similar reading levels are paired up for about 20–30 minutes per session. Each pair chooses a book or other form of reading material. From there, students negotiate how they will orally read the text together. Some pairs alternate pages, others read chorally as in paired reading, some read and reread one page at a time in echo fashion, and others combine ideas.

Lorraine encourages pairs to stop reading periodically, talk about what they have read, and ask questions of each other, especially when one student is having difficulty understanding the text. At the end of the session, buddies determine which pages in their shared book they will read at home that night. That way, they continue the reading silently and independently. Moreover, coordinating home reading makes each student feel responsible to his or her partner.

Lorraine feels that buddy reading leads to more reading, both in school and at home. "It really helps students see that reading is a social activity and creates some continuity between school and home reading." She also feels that it helps her keep track of her students' reading and engage in more meaningful reading conferences. "When I hear them reading aloud, I have a better sense of the content they are covering and it is easier for me to chat with them about their books."

How to Use Recorded Reading

If you would like to try paired reading but don't have the necessary support in the classroom or at home, try recording the passages you want students to work on. Give students selections from my Fluency Library and other material on audiotape or CD, and allow them to listen to the recordings while reading aloud a printed version of the text. A strong body of research from the United States and New Zealand supports this approach to fluency and reading development.

I suggest developing a listening center in which you provide students with the equipment, texts, and recordings of the texts so that they can read while listening to and being supported by the passage read to them. This center can easily be incorporated into the Repeated Reading Center (see page 40).

Recorded readings are simple to develop. Choose material from the Fluency Library and record 10- to 15-minute segments of the text in as fluent language as possible. Read at a natural pace, but if you are intending the recording center to be used by students who are not strong in fluency, try reading at a slightly slower pace to accommodate them.

Then, organize the recorded reading center for students to use. I recommend having students come to the center 3–5 times per week for 15- to 20-minute periods. During that time, students should practice the recorded passages while listening to them on tape. They should continue practicing until they are able to read the passage fluently themselves. At that point, students should read to you or record their best reading to be listened to by you at a later time.

One interesting twist on the development of a recorded reading center is to have students develop the recorded materials. If you are a fifth-grade teacher, you may wish to volunteer some of your students to develop recorded material for the third-grade class. Include your least-fluent readers in this task. They will have to practice third-grade materials (the level that may actually be their instructional reading level) until they can read them fluently—with good expression and pace. (Your fifth graders won't be embarrassed to read third-grade material because they have a real purpose for doing so.) Thus, your fifth graders benefit from creating the recorded materials, while the third graders benefit from the ever-growing body of recorded third-grade material being supplied to them.

How to Use Radio Reading

Have you ever listened closely to a radio show host or announcer? People in these positions must speak and read with superb fluency. Radio reading is a form of repeated reading that uses radio performances as the model. It was developed as a more collaborative alternative to round-robin reading, the archaic form of small-group instruction where the teacher chooses students to read aloud "on the spot" from an assigned text, without the benefit of practice. As such, students' readings are often disfluent, inexpressive, uninspired, and filled with word-recognition errors. Performances like these do little for the group's enjoyment of reading and even less for the reader's fluency and self-confidence.

During radio reading, groups of four to six students read aloud an assigned text in parts. But rather than calling on students during the session, you assign reading parts the day before. I prefer to use passages from texts that the group has already read silently. That way, students are familiar with the meaning and outcome of the passage. You can also use an unfamiliar text, but be sure to provide students with a detailed overview of it before trying radio reading.

When assigning parts, use good judgment based on what you know about your students as readers. Assign the longest or most challenging parts to students most able to handle them. You might also want to give a mini-lesson on the importance of reading with meaningful expression, just as radio and television announcers do. Emphasize that the only way to be able to read with good expression is through practice.

Once you've assigned each student a part, have him or her practice reading it aloud. Provide class time for individual practice and cooperative repeated reading (see page 41). Students can also practice their reading at home.

From there, ask each student to prepare two questions about his or her part—one literal (the answer can be found directly in the text) and one inferential (finding the answer requires the reader to use the information from the text, as well as his or her own background knowledge). Here are examples from Vera Williams's *A Chair for My Mother*:

Literal: Why did the girl in the story want to buy a chair?
Inferential: Do you think the girl and her family like the chair they bought? How do you know?

On the following day, have students gather into their groups and present their parts one by one, in the appropriate order. I sometimes ask students to come to the front of the group, stand tall, and read to the group as if they were giving a formal presentation. On other occasions, I have students choose the place to read.

Ask students to read as expressively and meaningfully as possible, as if they were professional announcers. I find that a fake microphone on a stand or an old radio is a good prop for reminding students of that point. If a student misreads a word, give her an opportunity to correct it. If she can't, you (and not the other students) should provide the correct word and ask her to continue, thus minimizing the disruption. The student may also call on you for help with particular words or phrases. Again, supply the word or phrase, and urge her to continue reading. As in paired reading, you may wish to make note of words that give students difficulty. Those words can be the focus of a quick mini-lesson after the radio reading session. The students who are not reading should either read along silently in the book or listen attentively with their books closed.

After all students have presented their parts, have them ask their literal and inferential questions in a follow-up discussion. Monitor the discussion, encouraging students to elaborate on questions and responses, and find quotes from the text to illustrate or justify their points. Here are some questions you might ask students to help them elaborate:

> *That's an interesting question. How did you come up with it?*

> *Tell us more about this character. Does he remind you of anyone you know or have read about?*

Teaching Tip

Record radio readings so that students can analyze them later. Save the very best recordings and play them as models for future reading groups that are assigned the same text. This way groups can try to "outperform" the recorded performance!

After the discussion, ask students to summarize the reading, their oral presentations, and what they need to work on for their next radio reading session.

Teaching Radio Reading

The Day Before Radio Reading

▶ Choose a passage with excerpts long enough to be read by four to six students, either from your regular reading program (the basal reader) or from a trade book included in the Fluency Library. Choose a selection that has already been read silently. If the selection has not been previously read, be sure to give students a detailed overview of the selection.

▶ Provide students with a mini-lesson on the importance of reading aloud with expression and meaning, using radio and television announcers as examples of people who do it well.

▶ Assign one part of the passage to each student. Give the most challenging parts to students who are best able to handle them. Assignments do not need to be equal in length.

▶ Have students practice reading their parts orally, alone or with others, in school and at home.

▶ Ask each student to develop two questions about his or her part: a literal, fact-based question and an inferential question that requires students to use information from the text and their background knowledge to arrive at an answer.

The Day of Radio Reading

▶ Remind students about the need to read with expression and meaning.

▶ Provide props such as a microphone or radio to lend authenticity to the experience.

▶ Have students read their assigned parts orally in the correct sequence.

▶ If students encounter problems while reading, provide help or allow them to call on you for help. Deal with the difficulty quickly to minimize disruption.

▶ After all the readings are complete, have students discuss the entire passage, using the questions they prepared the day before.

▶ At the end of the discussion, have students summarize the story, critique their reading, and make suggestions for the next radio reading.

How to Use Mumble Reading

Mumble reading allows many students to do repeated readings simultaneously, without disturbing other students. It was originally described by James Hoffman as part of his Oral Recitation Lesson. The students (or the teacher) select a passage of 50 to 100 words from their assigned reading material. Then students spend five minutes practicing reading their passages in a soft and low voice. You monitor students' reading, giving feedback when appropriate and plenty of encouragement. After the practice period, students read their passage aloud to the teacher or to the entire reading group. The teacher or students can then provide positive and informative feedback.

How to Use "Say It Like the Character"

Reading fluently involves more than simply reading accurately and quickly. It also involves reading with expression as a way to project the text's meaning. While using Read It Like the Character, students get "inside" a book's characters by reading monologues, dialogues, and conversations orally. In order for Read It Like the Character to be done properly, readers must do two things: (1) think about the feelings and disposition of the character and (2) practice reading the assigned text in a way that reflects the character's feelings and personality. Listeners must make inferences about the characters based on the way the passage is orally read and interpreted.

To do Say It Like the Character, find passages that contain monologues, dialogues, or conversations between multiple characters. They can be as short as one sentence or as long as a full page. My Fluency Library is filled with books that contain the voices of many different characters. If the story from which the passage comes is unfamiliar, give students some background so they understand the events and emotions leading up to the passage.

Have students practice reading the passage both silently and orally. Then read aloud a portion of it in several tones of voice (e.g., angry, delighted, confused, surprised), and talk about the feelings that can be inferred. Talk with students about how you created meaning with your voice.

Once students get the idea, have them try it on their own with a new passage. You can assign them a feeling to portray in their reading or let them choose their own. Have them practice the reading and then perform it, one at a time, in small groups. The students listening must guess the emotion that the reader is trying to portray. Following the reading, have students discuss what the reader did to convey the intended emotion (for example, increased or decreased volume or pitch, changed rate, dramatic pause, emphasis on a particular word) as well as the markers in the text itself (for example, italics, boldface print, illustrations) that gave clues to what the character was feeling.

Poetry works well for Say It Like the Character, too. I often give two or more students the same poem to read aloud, along with an emotional context from which to develop their reading, such as "You just won the lottery" or "You just found out that your best friend is moving away." Students practice their reading at home and then present it the next day. This becomes a dramatic example of how, in reading, meaning is not only conveyed by the written words but also by the way the words are presented by the reader.

Once students have practiced with several passages chosen by you, allow them to choose their own. In fact, a nice extension to Say It Like the Character is to have students write their own brief monologues or dialogues. When reading a passage as a group, stop at an appropriate point and ask students, *What is this character thinking right now?* Give students a few minutes to write a brief monologue, reminding them that they need to write in the voice of the character whose point of view they are representing. Then have students exchange their monologues with classmates, practice the monologue they receive for a few minutes, and then read it in character. The same process can be done with dialogues and conversations between multiple characters.

The process of creating and performing these monologues involves comprehension of characters, writing with voice, and fluency development through repeated readings and performance. Take it from me—this activity is a winner!

How to Use a Repeated Reading Center

Research confirms that repeated reading is one of the most powerful tools for developing fluency, including both automaticity in word recognition and expression or prosody in oral reading. In the same way that musicians practice to develop fluency or mastery in the musical composition they perform, readers must practice to develop mastery over texts they are expected to read. And just as practice of a specific musical composition generalizes to improvements in other pieces of music, sometimes more difficult than the one practiced, repeated readings of texts lead to improvements in the reading of that text and generalizes to other texts that also might be more difficult than the practiced one.

I would love to see a repeated reading center in every classroom in the country. I think of a repeated reading center as a kind of rehearsal room, a place where students can go to practice reading a passage or passages that they will later be asked to perform for others. The repeated reading center should be a place where students can read a text orally without disturbing other students. Thus, a corner of the classroom or even an area outside the classroom would be ideal locations for the center. Some teachers have created "rolling rehearsal centers" in which a wheeled cart that contains the materials necessary for the center can be rolled out into the school hallway or some other quiet area where students can practice without disturbing others and without being disturbed.

Few materials are necessary for a repeated reading center. Books and other materials that lend themselves to practice and performance are a must. Books from my Fluency Library make good additions to the repeated reading center. Tape recorders or other devices for recording students' voices for later listening and evaluation should be available. The recording equipment can also be used for students to listen to prerecorded versions of materials they are rehearsing to give them additional support while they rehearse. I think that record sheets and rating rubrics (perhaps in the form of individual fluency journals) that allow students to record the number of times they practiced a piece and to also rate and evaluate their own reading will help students manage their own practice. A graffiti wall on which students can write and display interesting words they have come across in their practice will help nurture a sense of word consciousness that is so important for readers and writers. Finally, consider the use of dividers that can isolate readers from visual and oral distractions as they practice a passage by themselves or with a partner or small group.

How to Use Cooperative Repeated Reading

Cooperative repeated reading has been shown to improve students' reading fluency and general reading skills (Koskinen & Blum, 1984; 1986). Using a 10- to 15-minute period during guided or independent reading, students work with a classmate or two on a short passage. Passages usually come from the basal text or a trade book that is being used in guided reading. To do cooperative repeated reading, follow these steps:

1. Have partners find a quiet, comfortable spot in the room for reading. Give each student a copy of the Cooperative Repeated Reading Response Form. (See TRCD BLM #04.)

2. Have one student read her passage to her partner(s) three times. Ask the partner(s) to listen and provide assistance where necessary. The partner(s) should also give feedback on the reading, based on the response sheet's criteria.

3. Have students reverse roles and repeat step 2.

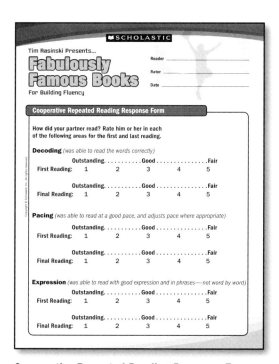

Cooperative Repeated Reading Response Form

How to Use Reader's Theater

Script reading is a form of performance reading that requires practice. When most teachers think of script reading, however, they think of putting on plays and all that goes with it: memorizing lines; learning movements; and creating costumes, props, and scenery, all of which require a lot of time. In classrooms, time is a precious commodity. Devoting time to staging plays takes time away from reading and other subject areas. Therefore, many teachers choose not to put on plays.

Fortunately, there is another type of script reading that is more manageable: reader's theater. In reader's theater, students stand in front of an audience, usually made up of their classmates, and read from scripts, which they hold in their hands or set on music stands. No costumes, props, or scenery are required unless the teacher and students wish to include them. Very little, if any, movement is involved. In a sense, reader's theater is a minimalist form of play performing.

Without movement, costumes, props, or scenery, the performers have only one attribute to make their performance meaningful and satisfying: their voices. And to use their voices well, performers need to practice the text beforehand.

Reader's theater is an authentic, entertaining, and educationally powerful way to read and communicate meaning. When implemented properly, it offers many opportunities for students to practice reading in multiple and meaningful ways. (See page 47 for guidelines on implementing reader's theater.)

We are seeing increasing evidence from classroom research that repeated reader's theater yields improvements in students' word recognition, fluency, and comprehension. Martinez, Roser, and Strecker (1999), for example, implemented a reader's theater curriculum in two second-grade classrooms over a ten-week period. Claire Carter and Ed Meneses, the teachers in the study, divided their classes into three "repertory groups" of six to nine students. On Mondays, each repertory group was given a different script to learn for the week. The scripts were developed from trade books. The teacher read the books expressively to the class on the first day of the week and then gave a brief mini-lesson on some aspect of fluency, such as reading to express the character's feelings, adjusting reading pace, pausing at the end of sentences, reading with appropriate volume, or emphasizing individual words or phrases. Then the scripts were distributed to the repertory groups—two copies to each student, one for practice at school and one for home.

The teachers provided 30 minutes per day to reader's theater instruction. On Tuesdays through Thursdays, students practiced all parts of the scripts, received feedback, auditioned for parts, and were assigned roles. They discussed the meaning of the text and any issues related to staging the performance. They were also encouraged to practice the scripts at home. Over the course of the week, students read their scripts 15 to 20 times!

Fridays were performance days. The groups read their scripts for a live audience made up of classmates, schoolmates, parents, the school principal, and other school personnel. The class was motivated to perform for a real audience. Claire Carter noted, "The audience effect was important. The anticipation of an audience is what made reading practice seem like a dress rehearsal."

The researchers measured students' reading performance prior to the project and at its conclusion ten weeks later. They also tracked the performance of two similar second-grade classrooms that received instruction with the same books, but without reader's theater. During the ten-week period, the reader's theater classrooms exhibited a fluency gain of 17 words per minute in reading unrehearsed text. The comparison classrooms made less than half that gain in their fluency—fewer than seven words per minute.

The authors also administered informal reading inventories before starting and ten weeks later at the end of the reader's theater program to determine overall progress in reading, including comprehension, from the implementation of reader's theater. Among the 28 students in the reader's theater classrooms, many students made gains of two grade levels. On average, students gained approximately 1.1 years during the ten-week study. Among the 28 students in the comparison classrooms, average gain was less than half of what was found in the reader's theater classrooms.

Some of the most compelling evidence came from the journals that students kept during the study. Omar wrote, "Reader's theater is the funnest reading I've ever did before!" Lucia wrote, "I never thought I could be a star, but I was the BEST reader today."

The teachers offered their own thoughts on the power of reader's theater. Claire Carter wrote about the pervasive power that the scripts and the practice of those scripts had on students' reading and writing: "They read those [original] books during their reading time. They wrote about the work and their own plays based on the same characters. They wrote story extensions of the scripts . . . . [They] repeatedly asked, 'Is it time for Reader's Theatre?'" The authors concluded that reader's theater "promoted oral reading fluency, as children explored and interpreted the meaning of literature with joy!"

Although reader's theater is often thought of as a primary grade activity, Worthy and Broaddus (2002) remind us that it can also be applied in the upper grades for developing fluency and promoting thoughtful, enjoyable engagements with texts.

After hearing about the success of the second-grade students in the Martinez, Roser, and Strecker study, fourth-grade teacher Lorraine Griffith decided to try it out during the better part of the 2000–2001 school year. She followed a format similar to the researchers': Monday introduction of scripts and performance texts, Tuesday through Thursday practice, Friday performance. She was amazed at the results. Her five Title I students made average gains of three grade levels during the year, and her entire class passed the state mandated proficiency examination in reading, which had not happened in previous years.

Lorraine attributed the success to reader's theater and the repeated reading that it requires. As students became familiar with the rich vocabulary and interesting sentences and phrases in the scripts, they began to try out the words and techniques in their own writing.

Title I teacher Lisa Samuda knows the benefits of repeated reading, but she has struggled with implementing it in her own pull-out program, in which she sees small groups of students for 30 minutes per day, three to five times per week. Lisa has developed her own innovative approach for using reader's theater. She finds out from the classroom teacher what her students have read, are reading, or will be reading for guided reading instruction. Then, either on her own or with her students (if the students have already read the story), she develops the text, or a portion of the text, into a script and makes enough copies for her students to read with her during instruction time and at home. Over the course of the next several days, they practice their script. Then, when they feel they have mastered it, the students return to their classroom where they perform their script for their classmates. It is a real motivator for these students, who are often viewed as the lowest performers, to become the stars every week or two. According to Lisa, "I have kids who read well come up to me and ask how they can get into my Title I class!"

> **Teacher-Created Scripts.** You can also create scripts yourself, and trade books are a great source of inspiration. Many trade books are written in script form; students can read directly from the book during performances. In most cases, however, you'll need to adapt the text.

Think of the published material that you share with students in read-aloud or guided reading—trade books, poems, speeches, and so forth. How might they be used or adapted for reader's theater? Stories with interesting characters, lively dialogue, and interesting problems work best. As I mentioned earlier, the scripts should not be too long, so if you're considering a lengthy story or chapter book, think about adapting only a portion of it.

Student-Created Scripts. If we can adapt texts for reader's theater, students should be able to as well. In fact, having students create their own scripts is a natural extension of reader's theater. It's a wonderful response activity after they have read or heard a story. For those who may disagree, who may think turning a story into a script is an inauthentic writing activity, remember that Hollywood is filled with scriptwriters who adapt novels for the screen every day—and get paid very well for doing it.

Many trade books can be transformed by students into reader's theater scripts. When students turn stories into scripts, it is a variable scaffolding experience. In other words, the original text acts as a model or support for student writers. To write their script, students must analyze deeply the well-formed writing of the author. They need to emulate the work of a good writer. This is a "variable" form of scaffolding because students can rely as heavily or lightly as they wish on the original story. Novice or struggling writers may not wish to deviate much from the original text. They may retain most of the original text but turn it into script form. More advanced or ambitious writers often take more liberties—adding, changing, and deleting characters and dialogue, changing scenes, and so on. Regardless of how close to or how far from the original text students stay or stray, the original text acts as a scaffold that supports their writing—a scaffold that students can go back to again and again for ideas, inspirations, and models.

Reader's Theater: A Weekly Plan

Following are some basic guidelines for doing reader's theater.

Before the Week Begins:

Select or write a script to be performed. Make a copy for each member of the repertory group.

Monday:

Introduce or review the nature, purpose, and procedures for reader's theater with the class.

Assign students to individual parts by having them volunteer or audition. Parts can be also assigned by students within groups and can rotate from one performance to another.

Tuesday–Thursday:

Have students practice their parts on their own, in their groups, in school, and at home.

Friday:

Invite students to perform their scripts for an audience (usually their classmates), but others can be invited as well—schoolmates, parents, the principal, and so on. Try to make the performance a special event. Many teachers I know turn Friday afternoons into a "classroom reader's theater festival" at which many repertory groups perform their scripts.

How to Use Poetry Performances

Poems, like scripts and speeches, are meant to be read aloud. Meaning is carried in the oral interpretation as well as in the words. And reading poetry has many benefits. The rhyme, rhythm, and repetition that pervade poetry, the elements that make reading it easy and fun, also serve to build fluency (Perfect, 1999). Most children have had experience with poetry even before entering school, so they are familiar with its characteristics. Moreover, the brevity of most poems makes them especially appropriate for multiple readings.

Kathy Perfect (1999), a fourth-grade teacher, notes that the best way to teach poetry is to live it and experience it daily in the classroom: "I strongly believe in immersing children daily in poetry of all kinds—rhymed and free verse, serious or silly—to help make poetic language both familiar and provocative. In my classroom, poetry begins our day, but it is never routine. Some days, on goes a mouse finger puppet that scoots across the top and down the sides of the book as I read poems from *Mice Are Nice* (Larrick, 1990). Other times, I might have one of the children put a hand puppet on while I read. But most of the time, it's just me, the poetry, and my class. I allow the reading of it to pull us in."

Each day Kathy allots time to share poems that connect to the time of year, current events, areas of study, or the general mood of the class. Students are invited to share their favorite poems at this time—poems they've practiced. Impromptu poetry breaks happen often, too, during which time Kathy and students may share a just-discovered poem. Group performances are also a regular feature of her reading program.

Several of my teacher acquaintances, in primary through middle grades, catapult their classrooms back to the 1950s and 1960s when poetry performances were held in coffeehouses. (Today, these performances go by another name: poetry slams.) Every Friday afternoon, during the last hour or so of the day, they stage a "poetry coffeehouse" or "poetry party." Students prepare by spending some time on Monday morning listening to their teachers read poems, browsing through the poetry collections in the room, and selecting one, two, or more poems to learn. At the coffeehouse, most poems are read by individual students, but some are read by pairs, trios, and larger groups. And there are always one or two poems that the whole class reads in choral style.

Students practice their selected poems throughout the week—in the classroom, during recess, after school, and at home. The teacher usually provides time for listening to and coaching students in their readings.

When late Friday afternoon arrives, lights are lowered, shades are drawn, and a couple of table lamps are lit to create just the right mood. A stool sits in the middle of the classroom "stage." A volunteer parent arrives with refreshments, usually hot chocolate, cider, chips, and cookies. Then the festivities begin.

The teacher (a.k.a. the master of ceremonies) calls the coffeehouse to order. She begins with her own selection and introduces the performers for the day. Students come up one by one and read their selections, knowing the key to a successful performance lies not only in the poet's words but also in their interpretation of those words. Between sets, students often talk about the performances. In one classroom, bongos and tambourines mysteriously appeared to accompany the readings and provide musical interludes between readings.

Visitors are always welcome to the event. The school principal, parents, and other teachers often show up. The cost of admission: a poem to share with the audience, of course. After all the poems have been recited—individually, in pairs, in small groups and large—and the refreshments consumed, the day ends, and students go home fortified with the power of poetry.

I'm continually amazed at the seriousness students give to coffeehouses. One of my most vivid memories involves a struggling fourth grader who, one cold afternoon in January with the wind blowing and snow falling, read his father's favorite poem, "The Cremation of Sam McGee" by Robert Service, a poem about life in the frigid Canadian Yukon during the Gold Rush, which attracted some unusual characters. This youngster awed his classmates by reading with amazing conviction and expression. He received the loudest applause (and finger snapping) of the day. This student, who had not met with much success as a reader before, learned that day how reading has the power to transform.

After observing these classroom coffeehouses over several years, I have noticed an interesting pattern. In September, students are most likely to choose silly poems by the likes of Shel Silverstein and Jack Prelutsky. By mid-year, students are guided by their teachers to more serious and thoughtful poetry. For example, last year, during the centennial of Langston Hughes's birth, one classroom of fourth graders spent January studying, reading, and performing the poetry from the Harlem Renaissance. Toward the end of the year, students eagerly write their own poetry, so the coffeehouses begin to feature a combination of published and original work. This is a very exciting evolution to witness.

Interestingly, most of the teachers deny teaching poetry in the traditional way. Instead, they use poetry as a vehicle for studying the richness of language and human creativity. They and their students use poetry coffeehouses as a vehicle for celebrating what they learn. The fact that students grow to love poetry and write their own is a natural outcome of this immersion.

How to Make Home Involvement in Fluency Work (Fast Start)

Research indicates that parental or home involvement is a key to students' success in learning to read. In fact, an international study of reading achievement found that parental involvement in children's reading was the number one predictor of reading achievement worldwide.

With that in mind, my colleague Nancy Padak and I developed a program called *Fast Start* (published by Scholastic). The program incorporates the basic principles of reading fluency instruction—modeling fluent reading for students, providing support for students while reading, giving students opportunities to practice reading passages with fluency and eventually perform what they practice, and providing opportunities to closely examine words within the passage that was practiced.

Fast Start is actually the way I taught my two youngest children to read. Thus, Nancy and I originally aimed Fast Start at students in kindergarten through early second grade, since the parents of those students are more predisposed to be involved in and concerned about reading. Moreover, we felt that if parents were invited to participate in their children's literacy development during their early school years, they would be more likely to remain involved later on. That said, the basic principles of Fast Start can easily be adapted for children in upper grades.

At the heart of Fast Start is a mantra that has guided much of my work: Good oral reading instruction involves *reading to children, reading with children,* and *listening to children read.* And that is exactly what we ask parents to do: devote 15 minutes to doing Fast Start with their children. (See TRCD BLM #08 for reproducible guidelines for parents.) Provide parents with a copy of a text every day—a short, lively poem, song, or excerpt from a story that contains a strong sense of author or character voice.

Getting parents involved with and committed to Fast Start is essential. Sending home the guidelines is a good start. I would also suggest that you hold a parent training session early in the school year where you explain the Fast Start program and demonstrate it for parents. Have parents and their children sign a copy of the enclosed "contract" before they leave the session. Give them a copy, and display the original on a bulletin board to remind students to do Fast Start with their parents. Throughout the school year, you might want to send home notes to parents reminding them about the importance of the daily Fast Start lesson at home. And, of course, parent-teacher conferences are always a good time to remind parents about doing Fast Start daily with their children.

Although it's simple and quick, Fast Start is effective, and research I have conducted with colleagues has been remarkably positive. In one study, we found that first-grade struggling readers who did ten minutes of Fast Start with their parents nightly made approximately twice the progress in word recognition and reading fluency than struggling first graders who received the same instruction in school but did not do Fast Start with their parents. Similar improvements can be found with older students by adapting the Fast Start routine for their use. All this requires is finding more appropriate passages for older students.

Steps for Parents Doing "Fast Start" at Home

▶ Parent and child sit side by side. The parent begins by reading the passage to the child several times, slowly, clearly, and expressively, pointing to the words in the text as she reads. After several readings, the child and parent read the passage aloud together, again pointing to the words. Parent and child should take time throughout the lesson to talk about the passage, its meaning, and their reading of it.

▶ After several readings by parent and child, the parent invites the child to read the text to her, again pointing to the words as he reads. The child should read the passage several times. The parent should listen attentively, offer support, and, most important, lavish praise on the child for good reading.

▶ The final part of the lesson involves word study. We want students to recognize words from the passages read with parents and in other texts they read. Parents can do word studies in several ways. For example, the child and parent can choose two to four interesting or challenging words from the passage and add them to the child's word bank, a collection of words on index cards, or to a home word wall that is simply a sheet of construction paper where the words are written. Those words can be practiced, sorted in various ways (e.g., by number of syllables, sound, meaning, etc.), and used for a variety of word games such as Word Bingo.

▶ The parent and child can also look for rhyming words and key word families (e.g., -ant, -ay, -ess) and write them on a blank sheet of paper. Then they can brainstorm and write other words from the same word family. These new words should be read several times and added to the word bank. This is a natural ending point for the lesson. Because the poem is short, the parent can encourage more repeated reading if the child shows interest.

(Informed teachers take advantage of this home reading by returning to the passage the next day and engaging students in five minutes of repeated reading, following it up with a few minutes of additional word study.)

How to Build Fluency Through Phrasing

The hallmark of disfluent reading is the word-by-word staccato-like reading that we so often hear in elementary classrooms. Some teachers call it robot reading, and others refer to it as machine gun reading. No matter what it is called, this type of reading is not enjoyable for the reader or the listener, and it will have a negative impact on comprehension.

Fluent reading, on the other hand, is marked by reading the words in phrase groups or chunks—noun phrases, verb phrases, prepositional phrases. When reading connects written discourse, meaning is more likely to be embedded in the phrase rather than in any individual word. Words like *if, of, and, the,* and *but* have very little meaning unless connected to a phrase. The sentence *He eats shoots and leaves.* can have quite different meanings depending on how it is phrased by the reader.

Chunks of words carry the meaning in text. And those chunks tend to be marked not only by appropriate pausing but also through expression. Readers (and speakers) will often lower their voice and extend the last sound of a phrase or sentence. Read the preceding sentence slowly and aloud. You will probably find that as you came to the end of a phrase or the end of the sentence, your voice dropped slightly, and you may have drawn out the last sound of the words *speakers, voice, sound,* and *sentence.* This was a way to chunk your reading at these points. Phrasing is important, and learning to read with appropriate expression will help readers learn to phrase text in meaningful ways. Several years ago, I reviewed the research literature on phrasing and found that a significant number of studies reported that when students were given direct instruction in phrasing, their fluency, comprehension, and overall reading achievement improved.

Using the Fluency Library to Improve Phrasing

The Fluency Library is an ideal body of literature for focusing students' attention on the role of phrasing in reading. Rhythmical texts such as poetry and song lyrics depend on proper phrasing, and texts written with strong voice also need to be read with good phrasing and expression. There are several ways you can use short texts or text segments to work on phrasing with students.

The first, of course, involves modeling appropriately phrased reading. When you read some of the books from my library (or other sources) to students, occasionally talk with students about how you read in phrases. You may wish to display a couple of sentences from the book you are reading for all the students to see and demonstrate how you were able to make meaning by phrasing the sentences appropriately. You may also wish to read some of the sentences or segments of the book in a choppy, monotonous voice or phrased at inappropriate places in the text. Ask students if they were able to understand what you were reading. Chances are that their understanding was severely restricted. Thus, the point you can make is that appropriate phrasing is important, not only for making the reading sound good but also for good comprehension.

Another simple but powerful way to develop phrasing skills involves you and your students selecting important phrases from books you or they are reading. Display the phrases on a word wall, and practice them whenever you have a few free minutes throughout the day—at the beginning of the school day, before and after lunch, or right before the end of the day. Not only will students practice reading authentic and meaningful phrases from passages they are reading or have recently read, but they will also practice many high-frequency words they need to learn until they are instantly recognizable. They will also be practicing, and hopefully talking about, the interesting words that will build their meaning vocabulary for reading and writing. Here are a few of the phrases (and short clauses and sentences) some primary-grade students and I selected after we had practiced and read the first half of *Click, Clack, Moo: Cows that Type* by Doreen Cronin.

Click, clack, moo

It was bad enough

Dear Farmer Brown

No milk today

We're closed.

In the background

They left a new note

Cried Farmer Brown

He heard them

Over the next two days we read the phrases, chanted the phrases, divided the group and read alternate lines, and talked about many of the words in the phrases. The phrases (and words) were explored for their meaning. Was Farmer Brown actually crying? What does *it was bad enough* mean? What does the word *background* mean? Other words such as *click, clack, dear,* and *Brown* were explored for their rhymes or word families. Still other words and phrases were simply enjoyed for their sound—the alliteration in *click, clack, moo,* and *new note* were pointed out. Soon, the phrases and words began to appear in students' conversations and in their writing. Every day or so we added a half-dozen phrases that we practiced and chatted about whenever we could.

All books by their very nature have interesting sentences and phrases to which we should draw students' attention, not only for the value in developing fluency but for the literary quality that we hope they will employ in their writing as well. Some books seem particularly well suited for this activity. Sharon Creech's *Love that Dog* and Libba Moore Gray's *My Mama Had a Dancing Heart,* for example, are written in beautiful and poignant phrases and short sentences that can and should be the object of student practice and examination.

Still another way to focus on phrasing is to type a page or two from any of the books that are part of the library, and print them out for students. Mark with a penciled slash the points where students should mark phrase boundaries in their reading—single slashes for within sentences and double slashes between sentences. Then, make a copy for every student in your reading group. Have them listen to you read the passage, then read it chorally as a group, and finally have them practice on their own or with a partner, always attending to appropriate phrasing and expression while reading.

A Chair for My Mother (page 1)

**My mother/works as a waitress/in the Blue Tile Diner.//
After school/sometimes I/go to meet her there.//Then/her
boss Josephine says,/"Good work,/honey,"/and pays me.//
And every time,/I put half/of my money/into the jar.//**

Dear Mr. Henshaw (pages 58–59)

January 19//

Dear Mr. Henshaw,//

Thank you/for sending me/the postcard/with the picture of/the lake and mountains/and all that snow.//Yes,/I will/continue to write/ in my diary/even if I do/have to pretend/I am writing/to you.//You know something?//I think/I feel better/when I write/in my diary.//

My teacher says/my writing skills/are improving.//Maybe/I really will/be a famous author/someday.//She said/our school/along with some other schools/is going to print/(that means mimeograph)/ a book of work/of young authors,/and I/should write a story for it.// The writers/of the best work/will win a prize-lunch/with a Famous Author/and/with winners/from other schools.//I hope/the Famous Author/is you.//

I don't/often get mail,/but today/I received/two postcards,/one from you/and one from Dad/in Kansas.//His said/he would phone me/sometime next week.//I wish/someday/he would have to/drive a load of something/to Wyoming/and would take me along/so I could get to meet you.//

That's all for now.//I am going/to try to think up/a story.//Don't worry.//I won't send it/to you/to read. I know you are busy/and I don't want/to be a nuisance.//

Your good friend,//

Leigh Botts/the First//

After students have practiced a passage for a few minutes, have them read it to you or a partner. (See samples provided on pages 56 and 57.) You or the partner should comment on the student's use of phrasing while reading. The entire lesson should take about 5–10 minutes.

The following day, have students read the very same passage from the original book or from copies that are not marked for phrase boundaries. Were they able to read with the same level of phrasing that they did the previous day? Were they able to attend to phrase boundaries even when the boundaries were not marked for them? The goal of the lesson is to have students transfer the skill they learned from practicing phrase-marked texts to passages that do not have the phrase boundaries explicitly marked.

As you and your students become comfortable and skilled in this mini-lesson, you may wish to have the students themselves mark the phrase boundaries of the texts you have chosen and copied. This gives them the opportunity to examine a passage thoughtfully for phrase boundaries they will use when practicing later.

Meaningful phrasing is critical to fluent and proficient reading, but it is rarely the focus of instruction. Using these simple instruction strategies along with the fine material in my Fluency Library will provide most students with all the help they need to discover the importance of phrasing and use that knowledge while they read.

How to Assess Students' Fluency

Reading assessment is important. If you want to provide the best instruction for your students, you have to know their strengths and weaknesses and the level at which they are reading. You also have to track their progress to know whether your instruction is having an impact. The *Three-Minute Reading Assessment* (Rasinski & Padak, 2005) book that comes with this program contains everything you need to assess all aspects of reading fluency and comprehension—in a matter of minutes.

Assessing Accuracy in Word Recognition/Decoding

Accurate word recognition is the foundation of fluency. Successful reading demands a certain level of accuracy in decoding words. The standard to indicate adequate decoding while reading a text is around 95% accuracy.

A range of 92–98% is generally referred to as the instructional level—the point at which a student can read the text with assistance, usually from a teacher. This is the level at which the reader is most likely to make greatest progress in reading because the text is not too easy and not too difficult. A 99% level of accuracy or better indicates independent reading level for that text: The text can be read successfully without assistance. Word recognition below 92% is the marker for frustration level. If the reader makes more than eight decoding errors for every 100 words, the text is most likely too difficult for him, even if assistance is provided.

To determine a student's level of accuracy, simply have her read a grade-level passage from the *Three-Minute Reading Assessment* book. A normally progressing student should read the passage at the instructional level (92–98%).

Assessing Automaticity in Word Recognition/Decoding

Automaticity in word recognition, a component of fluency, is usually measured in terms of reading rate. Students who are able to read the words in a grade-level passage at an appropriate rate for their grade level and the time of year provide evidence that they are developing their ability to recognize words automatically or effortlessly.

The *Three-Minute Reading Assessment* book provides you with the materials and means to assess students' automaticity in word recognition development. Simply have students read a grade-level passage orally. Mark any uncorrected errors they make as well as where they are in the text at the end of one minute. It's a good idea to record each student's reading for later analysis. Determine the number of words read correctly for each student, and compare it against the range of reading rates for each grade level and time of year that is found in the book. Again, you want your students to perform within the ranges appropriate for grade and time of year. Students who score at the lower end or below the lower boundary are candidates for additional instruction and intervention in fluency. Students who score well above the upper boundary may be reading too fast and may also be in need of additional instruction focused on reading at an appropriate rate to maximize comprehension.

Assessing Prosody/Expression in Reading

Prosody, or expressive reading, is the other half of reading fluency. Good readers read in such a way that their voices (even when reading silently) reflect meaning while reading. Readers make their voices sound as if they are making sense while they read. Research has shown that readers who read with good expression tend to read with good comprehension whether reading silently or orally. Thus, it is important to assess students' use of prosody when reading orally.

Again, the *Three-Minute Reading Assessment* makes it easy to assess prosody or expression. When students read the grade-level passage chosen for checking their word recognition accuracy and automaticity, you simply listen to their reading and determine if their oral expression sounds like authentic language; that is, read with good expression, volume, phrasing, pacing, and smoothness. To help you in this assessment, a fluency-expression rubric is included on page 11 of the *Three-Minute Reading Assessment*. As you listen to each student read, rate them from 1 to 4 in these four areas: expression and volume, phrasing and intonation, smoothness, and pace. The lowest score possible is a 4 and the highest is 16. Students who score above 8 are at a level of prosody appropriate for their grade level. Scores at or below 8 indicate that prosody may be a concern and may require additional instruction.

Assessing Comprehension

Reading comprehension is, of course, the ultimate goal of reading. Assessments of word-recognition accuracy, automaticity, and prosody would not be valid without requiring students to read for meaning. The *Three-Minute Reading Assessment* provides a quick and valid way for teachers to assess students' reading for meaning. After students have read the assigned grade-level passage (you may read it to students who are not sufficiently accurate or fluent to read it well on their own), they are asked to retell what they read.

As with the prosody component, the teacher's ability to determine a good level of understanding of a passage is used to assess comprehension. As the student recalls the passage for you, judge the quality of their retelling against the comprehension rubric that is provided on page 12 of the *Three-Minute Reading Assessment*. Well-organized, richly detailed retellings in which the student identifies the main thrust of the passage are given higher scores on the 6-point rubric. Less detailed retellings in which the main idea is not well stated or not stated at all are given lower scores. Scores of 4 and above indicate good progress in reading comprehension. Scores below 4 indicate that comprehension is a concern. And if poor comprehension scores are coupled with low scores in word recognition accuracy, automaticity, or prosody, it can be inferred that one cause of the poor comprehension is difficulties in any of these other areas.

Assessment needs to be valid and meaningful, and it also needs to be quick. I know teachers who complain about spending so much time doing the assessments mandated by their school administration that they have little time to teach the skills and strategies that are measured on the assessments they are giving. The *Three-Minute Reading Assessment* provides you with a simple, valid, and quick method for checking on your students' development in word recognition, fluency, and comprehension.

The brevity of the assessment also allows for it to be given several times over the course of the school year. I recommend that, at a minimum, the three-minute reading assessment be given to your students three times during the school year: at the beginning of the year to get baseline data, at midyear to make sure students are making appropriate progress, and at the end of the year to determine the progress made over a year's worth of instruction. Students who are not making appropriate progress or who are well behind in their reading development may need to be assessed even more often (e.g., monthly) or may require a more in-depth level of assessment provided by the school reading specialist or school psychologist.

Student performance on the assessments should be documented for easy analysis. Charts that you can use to record and analyze students' performance and progress in reading are included on pages 56–57 of the assessment guide. The first chart is for the entire class and allows you to chart progress over three separate assessments. The second chart allows you to record the reading development of individual students. Struggling students may require more thoughtful and detailed recording of their reading development. This chart allows you to make more detailed observations and commentary on those students.

Student Self-Assessment

It is important for students to be aware of their own development in reading fluency and reading skills in general. They need to become responsible for their own reading development. I feel that it is important for you to share the findings of your assessments with your students. Help them understand where they are doing well and where they need improvement. Students find it very fulfilling to know that they are making adequate progress in their reading.

The very same types of reading assessments just discussed can also be done by students. Older students in particular can easily be taught the methods for assessing one another's word recognition accuracy, automaticity, prosody, and comprehension. This will allow them to judge their own performance and development against their classmates' progress and to make self-determinations of what they need to do to become better readers.

I recommend the Multidimensional Fluency Scale (Fluency Expression rubric) for use with students. I encourage you to make a display version of the rubric for the classroom. Talk with your students about what each of the dimensions mean. Then encourage them to regularly rate their own reading for its prosodic quality, keeping track of progress in a personal journal or chart. This will help students develop the metacognitive awareness of their own reading that is so essential to and motivating for their own reading development. You might also want to have students assess your reading on the scale when you read aloud to the class. When you are purposefully (I hope) reading a text with less than desired fluency, are they able to detect it and score it appropriately? Such an activity makes for lively discussions on the nature of fluency and meaning and how fluency is developed.

Instruction is optimized when we know what to teach, whom to teach, the correct level of intensity to teach, and whether our instruction is having the desired effect. Assessment allows this to happen. As you work with my Fluency Library, I hope you will periodically use assessment to ensure that your students are making progress in increasing fluency and comprehension.

Book Charts

LIBRARY A	Genre	Modeled Reading
Abe Lincoln: The Boy Who Loved Books	Biography	Relate Text to Illustrations
Alexander and the Terrible, Horrible, No Good, Very Bad Day	Humor, Silliness	Expressive Reading
Apple Pie Tree, The	Picture Book	Punctuation Clues
Chair for My Mother, A	Realistic Fiction	Text Clues
Cinderella	Tales, Fairytale, Fractured, Modern	Return Sweep
CLICK, CLACK, MOO: Cows that Type	Humor, Silliness	Onomatopoeia/Alliteration
Come On, Rain	Poetry	Pace
Corduroy	Picture Book	Punctuation
Diary of a Worm	Humor, Silliness	Dates and Numbers
Five Little Monkeys Jumping on the Bed	Picture Book	Repetition and Variation
Frida	Picture Book, Biography	Punctuation Clues
How I Became a Pirate	Action, Adventure	Dialect
I Am the Dog, I Am the Cat	Picture Book	Typeface Clues
I Lost My Tooth in Africa	Picture Book	Punctuation Clues
I Stink!	Humor, Silliness	Typeface Clues
Is Your Mama a Llama?	Picture Book	Quotation Marks
K Is for Kissing a Cool Kangaroo	Alphabet Book	Rhythm
Let's Play in the Forest While the Wolf Is Not Around	Tales, Fairytale, Fractured, Modern	Choral Singing
Mañana, Iguana	Tales, Fairytale, Fractured, Modern	Foreign Words
Martin's Big Words: The Life of Dr. Martin Luther King, Jr.	Biography	Numbers and Dates
Million Fish . . . More or Less, A	Tales	Dialect
Mufaro's Beautiful Daughters	Tales, Fairytale, Fractured, Modern	Proper Nouns and Foreign Names
My Mama Had a Dancing Heart	Poetry	Hyphenated Words Pairs
Owl Moon	Picture Book	Tone
Ruby in Her Own Time	Picture Book	Punctuation Clues
Stone Soup	Tales, Fairytale, Fractured, Modern	Punctuation Clues
Subway Mouse, The	Picture Book	Dialogue
Tell Me a Story, Mama	Picture Book	Italics
Too Loud Lily	Picture Book	Typeface Clues
Web Files, The	Picture Book	Tone
What a Day It Was at School	Poetry	Rhyme
YO! YES?	Picture Book	Punctuation Clues

Individualized Practice	Fluency Performance (Writing)	Fluency Performance (Oral Presentation)
Echo Reading; Individual Echo Reading/Call-and-Response	Drawings with Speech Balloons	Dramatization
Say It Like the Character; Paired Reading/Echo Reading	Write a New Scene	Dramatization
Choral Reading; Buddy Reading/Echo Reading	Diagram	Read Aloud
Mumble Reading; Recorded Reading/Choral Reading	Diary Entries	Read Aloud
Choral Reading; Call-and-Response/Paired Reading	Story Map	Retelling
Refrain; Antiphonal Reading/Echo Reading	Letters	Deliver and Read
Choral Reading; Cumulative Choral Reading/Echo Reading	Description	Read Aloud
Monologue; Radio Reading/Echo Reading	Story Map	Puppet Theater
Cooperative Repeated Reading; Buddy Reading/Echo Reading	Diary of a Bug	Read Aloud
Choral Singing; Choral Singing/Refrain	Lyrics	Concert
Choral Reading; Recorded Reading/Call-and-Response	Self-Portraits	Guided Tour
Say It Like the Character; Buddy Reading/Choral Reading	Scripts	Act It Out!
Cooperative Repeated Reading; Buddy Reading/Impromptu Choral Reading	Script	Reader's Theater
Antiphonal Reading; Mumble Reading/Echo Reading	Personal Narrative	Read Aloud
Choral Reading; Impromptu Choral Reading/Read While Listening	Riddles	Guessing Game
Dialogue; Antiphonal Reading/Paired Reading	Sentence Frames	Share
Choral Reading; Recorded Reading/Mumble Reading	Alphabet Book	Read Aloud
Class Recording; Take Home Practice/Refrain	Dance and Movement	Musical Performance
Echo Reading; Dialogue/Choral Reading	Scripts	Reader's Theater
Cooperative Repeated Reading; Antiphonal Reading/Echo Reading	Personal Essay	Discussion
Dialogue; Buddy Reading/Echo Reading	Tall Tales	Storytelling Contest
Cooperative Repeated Reading; Mumble Reading/Read While Listening	Story Map	Retelling
Impromptu Choral Reading; Antiphonal Reading/Echo Reading	Memoir	Read Aloud
Impromptu Choral Reading; Choral Reading/Echo Reading	Nature Description	Read Aloud
Choral Reading; Radio Reading/Mumble Reading	Comic Strip	Read Aloud
Say It Like the Character; Dialogue/Choral Reading	What Happens Next?	Read Aloud
Say It Like the Character; Radio Reading/Choral Reading	Narrative	Storytelling
Say It Like the Character; Dialogue	Personal Narrative	Story Time
Cooperative Repeated Reading; Buddy Reading/Echo Reading	Dialogue	Performance
Refrain; Radio Reading/Reading While Listening	Scripts	Reader's Theater
Cumulative Choral Reading; Line-a-Child/Choral Reading	Poem	Poetry Conference
Dialogue; Mumble Reading/Dialogue	Comic Strip	Read Aloud

LIBRARY B	Genre	Modeled Reading
American Tall Tales	Tales, American Legend, Tall Tale	Analyze Characters/Intonation
Bad Beginning, The	Humor, Silliness	Read With Expression
Black Cat	Poetry	Phrasing
Catwings	Fantasy	Punctuation Clues
Charlotte's Web	Realistic Fiction	Using a Different Voice for Each Character
Clarice Bean Spells Trouble	Realistic Fiction	Character Analysis and Intonation
Cloudy with a Chance of Meatballs	Tales, Fractured, Modern	Pace and Phrasing
Cockroach Cooties	Realistic Fiction	Punctuation Clues
Dear Mr. Henshaw	Journal, Diary, Letters	Prosody
Firework-Maker's Daughter, The	Fable	Chunking
Granddaddy's Gift	Historical Fiction	Pace
Hey You! C'mere: A Poetry Slam	Poetry	Reading slang or ungrammatical text
In the Year of the Boar and Jackie Robinson	Historical Fiction	Punctuation Clues
It's Raining Pigs & Noodles	Poetry	Prosody
Kick in the Head, A	Poetry	Tone/Mood
More Than Anything Else	Biography, Historical	Italics
New Kid on the Block, The	Poetry	Rhyme
Nothing Ever Happens on 90th Street	Realistic Fiction	Punctuation Clues
Oh, Brother	Realistic Fiction	Punctuation Clues
Our Strange New Land: Elizabeth's Jamestown Colony Diary, Book One	Journal, Diary, Letters	Tone/Mood
Phoebe the Spy	Realistic Fiction	Emphasize Italic Words
Ramona the Pest	Realistic Fiction	Punctuation Clues
Red Riding Hood	Tales, Fairytale, Fractured, Modern	Reading Using Different Voices
Rosa	Biography, Historical	Intonation
Sarah, Plain and Tall	Historical Fiction	Punctuation Clues
Sidewalk Chalk: Poems of the City	Poetry	Phrasing
Stopping by Woods on a Snowy Evening	Rhyme, Rhyming Story	Phrasing
Talkin' About Bessie: The Story of Aviator Elizabeth Coleman	Biography, Historical	Prosody
Thank You, Mr. Falker	Autobiography	Punctuation Clues
True Story of the 3 Little Pigs, The	Tales, Fairytale, Fractured, Modern	Intonation
Uncle Jed's Barbershop	Historical Fiction	Chunking
Wings	Fantasy	Punctuation Clues

Individualized Practice	Fluency Performance (Writing)	Fluency Performance (Oral Presentation)
Dialogue; Dialogue/Paired Reading	Tall Tale	Read Aloud
Say It Like the Character; Radio Reading/Echo Reading	Letter to the Author	Readers' Panel
Choral Reading; Line-a-Child/Refrain	Lyrics	Rap
Dialogue; Radio Reading/Echo Reading	Illustrated Sequence	Shared Reading
Cooperative Repeated Reading; Say It Like the Character/Mumble Reading	Script	Reader's Theater
Say It Like the Character; Dialogue/ Read While Listening	Extension	Read Aloud
Cooperative Repeated Reading; Recorded Reading/Buddy Reading	Write a Forecast	Weather Report
Dialogue; Radio Reading/Echo Reading	Begin or End the Scene	Read Aloud
Buddy Reading; Buddy Reading/Choral Reading	Story Proposal	Writers' Conference
Choral Reading; Buddy Reading/Read While Listening	Draw Illustrations with Labels and Captions	Present Designs
Antiphonal Reading; Buddy Reading/Echo Reading	Analyze Characters	Discussion
Cooperative Repeated Reading; Recorded Reading/Buddy Reading	Poetry	Poetry Slam
Cooperative Repeated Reading; Buddy Reading/Mumble Reading	Postcards	Exchange
Line-a-Child; Impromptu Choral Reading	Poetry	Poetry Slam
Cumulative Choral Reading; Line-a-Child	Poetry	Poetry Slam
Read with Emphasis; Buddy Reading/Echo Reading	Tableau	Guessing Game
Impromptu Choral Reading; Line-a-Child/Choral Reading	Poetry	Poetry Slam
Paired Reading; Mumble Reading/Choral Reading	What if...?	Read Aloud
Paired Reading; Mumble Reading/Choral Reading	Begin or End the Scene	Read Aloud
Cooperative Repeated Reading; Buddy Reading/Echo Reading	Diary	Read Aloud
Say It Like the Character; Dialogue	Expand on the Passage	Perform a Dialogue
Cooperative Repeated Reading; Buddy Reading/Echo Reading	Dialogue	Awkward Conversations
Cooperative Repeated Reading; Say It Like the Character/Mumble Reading	Scripts	One-Kid-Show
Cooperative Repeated Reading; Say It Like the Character/Echo Reading	Scripts	Reader's Theater
Choral Reading; Recorded Reading/Read While Listening	Scripts	Reader's Theater
Paired Reading; Line-a-Child/Echo Reading	Poetry	Poetry Slam
Paired Reading; Line-a-Child/Echo Reading	Poetry	Poetry Slam
Cooperative Repeated Reading; Buddy Reading/Recorded Reading	News Report	Radio Broadcast
Cooperative Repeated Reading; Recorded Reading/Buddy Reading	Book Review	Book Talk
Say It Like the Character; Say It Like the Character/Read While Listening	Fairytale	Campfire Reading
Paired Reading; Mumble Reading/Read While Listening	Personal Essay	Read Aloud
Cooperative Repeated Reading; Echo/Buddy Reading	Scripts	Reader's Theater

LIBRARY C	Genre	Modeled Reading
Abby Takes a Stand	Historical Fiction	Reading Using Different Voices
Adam Canfield of the Slash	Realistic Fiction	Prosody
Al Capone Does My Shirts	Historical Fiction	Reading Dialogue
Ask Me No Questions	Realistic Fiction	Pace and Tone
Big Talk: Poems for Four Voices	Poetry	Prosody
Blood on the River: James Town 1607	Historical Fiction	Typeface Clues
Bull Run	Historical Fiction	Punctuation Clues
Crash	Realistic Fiction	Reading Dialogue
Dream Keeper and Other Poems, The	Poetry	Pace and Tone
Drums, Girls, & Dangerous Pie	Realistic Fiction	Punctuation Clues
Fields of Fury: The American Civil War	History	Punctuation Clues
Freedom Walkers: The Story of the Montgomery Bus Boycott	Biography, Historical	Phrasing and Pace
Heat	Realistic Fiction	Punctuation Clues
heaven	Realistic Fiction	Say It Like the Character
It's a Mall World After All	Realistic Fiction	Prosody
Life As We Knew It	Realistic Fiction	Chunking
Long Way from Chicago, A	Realistic Fiction	Pace
Love that Dog	Verse Novel	Pace and Phrasing
Out of the Dust	Verse Novel	Visualizing
Pink and Say	Historical Fiction	Reading Dialect
Poetry for Young People: American Poetry	Poetry	Expressive reading
Poetry for Young People: Emily Dickinson	Poetry	Phrasing
Poetry for Young People: Robert Browning	Poetry	Dialogue and Rhyme
Poetry for Young People: Robert Frost	Poetry	Line Punctuation/Phrasing in Poetry
Replay	Realistic Fiction	Dialogue
Rhyme and PUNishment	Poetry/Word Play	Phrasing
River Between Us, The	Historical Fiction	Pacing and Visualizing
Shakespeare Stealer, The	Historical Fiction	Prosody
Shh! We're Writing the Constitution	Historical Fiction	Chunking
Up Before Daybreak: Cotton and People in America	Primary Source	Reading Numbers and Dates
World Before This One, The: A Novel Told in Legend	Tales, Pourquoi Tale	Pace
Young Man and the Sea, The	Realistic Fiction	Typeface Clues

Individualized Practice	Fluency Performance (Writing)	Fluency Performance (Oral Presentation)
Cooperative Repeated Reading; Cooperative Repeated Reading/Echo Reading	Diary Entries	Performance Reading
Antiphonal Reading; Mumble Reading/Echo Reading	News Story	TV Broadcast
Say It Like the Character; Mumble Reading/Dialogue	Dialogue	Performance
Cooperative Repeated Reading; Buddy Reading/Echo Reading	Reminiscence	Performance Reading
Paired Reading Cumulative Choral Reading/Paired Reading	Poetry	Poetry Reading
Antiphonal Reading; Mumble Reading/Choral Reading	Dialogue	Performance Reading
Cooperative Repeated Reading; Cooperative Reading/Echo Reading	Letters	Performance Reading
Say It Like the Character; Mumble Reading/Echo Reading	Comic Strip	Reader's Theater
Antiphonal Reading; Recorded Reading/Antiphonal Reading	Blues Poem	Poetry Slam
Paired Reading; Mumble Reading	Dialogue	Performance
Cooperative Repeated Reading; Buddy Reading/Echo Reading	Sequential Paragraph	Performance
Paired Reading; Choral Reading/Echo Reading	Speeches	Performance Reading
Antiphonal Reading; Recorded Reading/Mumble Reading	Paragraph	Performance Reading
Cooperative Repeated Reading; Mumble Reading/Echo Reading	Letters	Performance Reading
Cooperative Repeated Reading; Mumble Reading/Echo Reading	Essay	Performance Reading
Cooperative Repeated Reading; Buddy Reading/Paired Reading	Myth or Legend	Campfire Storytelling
Antiphonal Reading; Buddy Reading/Paired Reading	Setting	Sketch to Stretch
Cumulative Choral Reading; Buddy Reading/Paired Reading	Poetry	Poetry Slam
Cumulative Choral Reading; Mumble Reading/Echo Reading	News Broadcast Script	Radio Theater
Say It Like the Character; Mumble Reading/Echo Reading	Dialogue	Performance Reading
Cumulative Choral Reading; Choral Reading/Echo Reading	Poem, paragraph, or monologue	Performance Reading
Cooperative Repeated Reading; Recorded Reading/Mumble Reading	Poem	Performance Reading
Antiphonal Reading; Cooperative Repeated Reading/Recorded Reading	Poetry	Storytelling
Paired Reading; Line-a-Child/Echo Reading	Haiku	Poetry Reading
Cooperative Repeated Reading; Say It Like the Character/Paired Reading	Script	Reader's Theater
Paired Reading; Line-a-Child/Reading While Listening	Puns	Rap
Cooperative Repeated Reading; Mumble Reading/Echo Reading	Portrait	Performance Reading
Buddy Reading; Buddy Reading /Antiphonal Reading	Narrative	Performance Reading
Cooperative Repeated Reading; Recorded Reading/Mumble Reading	Cartoon Dialogue	Performance Reading
Antiphonal Reading; Buddy Reading/Paired Reading	Informational Paragraph	Read Aloud
Antiphonal Reading; Buddy Reading/Echo Reading	What Happens Next?	Campfire Stories
Antiphonal Reading; Mumble Reading/Buddy Reading	Paragraph	Performance Reading

Resources for Fluency Instruction

Books

Fry, E., & Rasinski, T. (2007). *Increasing fluency with high-frequency word phrases grs. 1–3.* Huntington Beach, CA: Teacher Created Materials/Shell Publishing.

Johns, J., & Berglund, R. (2006). *Fluency: Strategies and assessments.* Dubuque, IA: Kendall Hunt.

Padak, N., & Rasinski, T. (2005). *Fast start for early readers: A research-based, send-home literacy program.* New York: Scholastic.

Padak, N., & Rasinski, T. (2007). *Evidence-based instruction in reading: professional development guide to fluency.* New York: Allyn & Bacon.

Rasinski, T. (2004). *Texts for fluency practice.* Huntington Beach, CA: Teacher Created Materials/Shell Publishing.

Rasinski, T. V. (2003). *The fluent reader: Oral reading strategies for building word recognition, fluency, and comprehension.* New York: Scholastic.

Rasinski, T. V. (2004). *Assessing reading fluency.* Honolulu: Pacific Resources for Education and Learning. Available at www.prel.org.

Rasinski, T., Blachowicz, C., & Lems, K. (2006). *Fluency instruction: Research-based best practices.* New York: Guilford.

Rasinski, T., & Brothers, K. (2005). *Poems for word study.* Huntington Beach, CA: Teacher Created Materials/Shell Publishing.

Rasinski, T. V., & Padak, N. D. (2001). *From phonics to fluency: Effective teaching of decoding and reading fluency in the elementary school.* New York: Longman.

Rasinski, T. V., & Padak, N. (2005). *Three-minute reading assessments: Word recognition, fluency, and comprehension for grades 1–4.* New York: Scholastic.

Rasinski, T. V., & Padak, N. (2005). *Three-minute reading assessments: Word recognition, fluency, and comprehension for grades 5–8.* New York: Scholastic.

Shepard, A. (2004). *Readers on stage: Resources for reader's theater (or readers theatre), with tips, play scripts, and worksheets, or how to do simple children's plays that build reading fluency and love of literature.* Shepard Publications.

Web Sites with Resources for Teaching Fluency

www.timrasinski.com

www.busyteacherscafe.com/units/fluency.htm

http://www.nifl.gov/partnershipforreading/publications/reading_first1fluency.html

http://content.scholastic.com/browse/article.jsp?id=4367

http://www.prel.org/products/re_/assessing-fluency.htm

http://content.scholastic.com/browse/article.jsp?id=4468

http://www.cldinternational.org/infosheets/fluency.asp

www.scholastic.com

References

Chard, D. J., Vaughn, S., & Tyler, B. (2002). A synthesis of research on effective interventions for building fluency with elementary students with learning disabilities. *Journal of Learning Disabilities, 35,* 386–406.

Duke, N. K., Pressley, M., & Hilden, K. (2004). Difficulties in reading comprehension. In C. A. Stone, E. R. Silliman, B. J. Ehren, and K. Apel (Eds.), *Handbook of language and literacy; Development and disorders,* pp. 501–520. New York: Guilford.

Griffith, L. W., & Rasinski, T. V. (2004). A focus on fluency: How one teacher incorporated fluency with her reading curriculum. *The Reading Teacher, 58,* 126–137.

Hoffman, J. V. (1987). Rethinking the role of oral reading in basal instruction. *Elementary School Journal, 87,* 367–373.

Hoffman, J. V., & Crone, S. (1985). The oral recitation lesson: A research-derived strategy for reading in basal texts. In J. A. Niles & R. V. Lalik (Eds.), *Issues in literacy: A research perspective, 34th Yearbook of the National Reading Conference,* pp. 76–83. Rockfort, NY: National Reading Conference.

Koskinen, P. S., & Blum, I. H. (1984). Repeated oral reading and acquisition of fluency. In J. A. Niles & L. A. Harris (Eds.), *Changing perspectives on research in reading/language processing and instruction, 33rd Yearbook of the National Reading Conference,* pp. 183–187. Rochester, NY: National Reading Conference.

Koskinen, P. S., & Blum, I. H. (1986). Paired repeated reading: A classroom strategy for developing fluent reading. *The Reading Teacher, 40,* 70–75.

Kuhn, M. R., & Stahl, S. A. (2000). *Fluency: A review of developmental and remedial practices* (CIERA Rep. No. 2-008). Ann Arbor, MI: Center for the Improvement of Early Reading Achievement.

LaBerge, D., & Samuels, S. A. (1974). Toward a theory of automatic information processing in reading. *Cognitive Psychology, 6,* 293–323.

Larrick, N. (Ed.) (1990). *Mice Are Nice.* New York: Philomel.

Martinez, M., Roser, N., & Strecker, S. (1999). "I never thought I could be a star": A Readers Theatre ticket to reading fluency. *The Reading Teacher, 52,* 326–334.

National Reading Panel. (2000). *Report of the National Reading Panel: Teaching children to read. Report of the subgroups.* Washington, D.C.: U.S. Department of Health and Human Services, National Institutes of Health.

Perfect, K. A. (1999). Rhyme and reason: Poetry for the heart and head. *The Reading Teacher, 52,* 728–737.

Rasinski, T. V., & Hoffman, J. V. (2003). Theory and research into practice: Oral reading in the school literacy curriculum. *Reading Research Quarterly, 38,* 510–522.

Rasinski, T. V., & Padak, N. (2001). *From phonics to fluency: Effective teaching of decoding and reading fluency in the elementary school.* New York: Addison Wesley Longman.

Rasinski, T. V., & Padak, N. D. (1998). How elementary students referred for compensatory reading instruction perform on school-based measures of word recognition, fluency, and comprehension. *Reading Psychology: An International Quarterly, 19,* 185–216.

Rasinski, T. V., Padak, N. D., Linek, W. L., & Sturtevant, E. (1994). Effects of fluency development on urban second-grade readers. *Journal of Educational Research, 87,* 158–165.

Reutzel, D. R., & Hollingsworth, P. M. (1993). Effects of fluency training on second graders' reading comprehension. *Journal of Educational Research, 86,* 325–331.

Reutzel, D. R., Hollingsworth, P. S., & Eldredge, L. (1994). Oral reading instruction: The impact on student reading achievement. *Reading Research Quarterly, 29,* 40–62.

Vacca, J., Vacca, R., & Gove, M. (2000). *Reading and learning to read.* New York: Allyn & Bacon.

Worthy, J., & Broaddus, K. (2002). Fluency beyond the primary grades: From group performance to silent, independent reading. *The Reading Teacher, 55,* 334–343.

Other Fluency-Related Resources

Allington, R. L. (1983). Fluency: The neglected goal of the reading program. *The Reading Teacher, 36,* 556–561.

Allington, R. L. (2000). *What really matters for struggling readers.* New York: Allyn & Bacon.

Anderson, R. C., Wilson, P. T., & Fielding, L. G. (1988). Growth in reading and how children spend their time outside of school. *Reading Research Quarterly, 23,* 285–303.

Aslett, R. (1990). *Effects of the oral recitation lesson on reading comprehension of fourth grade developmental readers. Unpublished doctoral dissertation.* Provo, UT: Brigham Young University.

Beach, S. A. (1993). Oral reading instruction: Retiring the bird in the round. *Reading Psychology, 14,* 333–338.

Bear, D., Invernizzi, M., Templeton, S., & Johnston, F. (2007). *Word their way: Word study for phonics, vocabulary, and spelling instruction* (4th ed.). New York: Prentice Hall.

Beck, I. (2005). *Making sense of phonics: The hows and whys (solving problems in teaching of literacy).* New York: Guilford.

Biggs, M., Homan, S., Dedrick, R., & Rasinski, T. (In press). Using an interactive singing software program: A comparative study of middle school struggling readers. *Reading Psychology, An International Quarterly.*

Biemiller, A. (1977). Relationships between oral reading rates for letters, words, and simple text in the development of reading achievement. *Reading Research Quarterly 13,* 223–253.

Blum, I. H., Koskinen, P. S., Tennant, N., Parker, E. M., Straub, M., & Curry, C. (1995). Using audiotaped books to extend classroom literacy instruction into the homes of second-language learners. *Journal of Reading Behavior, 27* (4), 535–563.

Bromage, B. K., & Mayer, R.E. (1986). Quantitative and qualitative effects of repetition on learning from technical text. *Journal of Educational Psychology, 78,* 271–278.

Carbo, M. (1978). Teaching reading with talking books. *The Reading Teacher, 32,* 267–273.

Carbo, M. (1978). A word imprinting technique for children with severe memory disorders. *Teaching Exceptional Children, 11,* 3–5.

Carbo, M. (1981). Making books talk to children. *The Reading Teacher, 35,* 186–189.

Carver, R. P. (1990). *Reading Rate: A Review of Research and Theory.* San Diego: Academic Press.

Carver, R. P., & Hoffman, J. V. (1981). The effect of practice through repeated reading on gain in reading ability using a computer-based instructional system. *Reading Research Quarterly, 16,* 374-390.

Chall, J. S. (1996). *Stages of reading development* (2nd ed.). Fort Worth, TX: Harcourt-Brace.

Chomsky, C. (1976). After decoding: What? *Language Arts, 53,* 288–296.

Clay, M. M. (1993). *Reading Recovery: A guidebook for teachers in training.* Portsmouth, NH: Heinemann.

Cunningham, P. M. (2004). *Phonics They Use* (4th ed.). New York: Allyn & Bacon.

Dahl, P. R. (1970). *An experimental program for teaching high speed word recognition and comprehension skills.* In J. E. Button, T. Lovitt, & T. Rowland (Eds.), *Communications research in learning disabilities and mental retardation,* pp. 33–65. Baltimore, MD: University Park Press.

Daane, M. C., Campbell, J. R., Grigg, W. S., Goodman, M. J., & Oranje, A. (2005). *Fourth-Grade Students Reading Aloud: NAEP 2002 Special Study of Oral Reading.* Washington, D.C.: U.S. Department of Education, Institute of Education Sciences.

Deno, S. L. (1985). Curriculum-based measurement: The emerging alternative. *Exceptional Children, 52,* 219–232.

Deno, S. L., Mirkin, P., & Chiang, B. (1982). Identifying valid measures of reading. *Exceptional Children, 49,* 36–45.

Dowhower, S. L. (1987). Effects of repeated reading on second-grade transitional readers' fluency and comprehension. *Reading Research Quarterly, 22,* 389–407.

Dowhower, S. L. (1994). Repeated reading revisited: Research into practice. *Reading and Writing Quarterly, 10,* 343–358.

Durkin, D. (1978). What classroom observations reveal about reading comprehension instruction. *Reading Research Quarterly, 14* (4), 482–533.

Ehri, L. C. (2005). Learning to read words: Theory, findings, and issues. *Scientific Studies of Reading, 9,* 167–188.

Eldredge, J. L. (1990). Increasing reading performance of poor readers in the third grade by using a group assisted strategy. *Journal of Educational Research, 84,* 69–77.

Eldredge, J. L., & Butterfield, D. D. (1986). Alternatives to traditional reading instruction. *The Reading Teacher, 40,* 32–37.

Eldredge, J. L., & Quinn, W. (1988). Increasing reading performance of low-achieving second graders by using dyad reading groups. *Journal of Educational Research, 82,* 40–46.

Eldredge, J. L., Reutzel, D. R., & Hollingsworth, P. M. (1996). Comparing the effectiveness of two oral reading practices: Round-robin reading and the Shared Book Experience. *Journal of Literacy Research, 28,* 201–225.

Florida Center for Reading Research. (2006). *Review of Fluency First.* Accessed at http://www.fcrr.org/FCRRReports/PDF/FluencyFirstR2.pdf on September 5, 2006.

Fowler, M. C., Lindemann, L. M., Thacker-Gwaltney, S., & Invernizzi, M. (2002). *A second year of one-on-one tutoring: An intervention for second graders with reading difficulties.* (CIERA Rep. No. 3-019). Ann Arbor, MI: Center for the Improvement of Early Reading Achievement.

Fry, E. (1998). The most common phonograms. *The Reading Teacher, 34,* 284–289.

Fry, E., & Kress, J. (2006). *The reading teacher book of lists* (5th ed.). San Francisco: Jossey-Bass.

Gaskins, I. W., Ehri, L. C., Cress, C. O., O'Hara, C., & Donnelly, K. (1996–2007). Procedures for word learning: Making discoveries about words. *The Reading Teacher, 50,* 312–327.

Good, R., & Kaminski, R. (2005). *Dynamic indicators or basic early literacy skills* (6th ed.). Eugene, OR: Institute for the Development of Educational Achievement.

Good, R., Simmons, D., & Kame'enui, E. (2001). The importance and decision-making utility of a continuum of fluency-based indicators of foundational reading skills for third-grade high-stakes outcomes. *Scientific Studies in Reading, 5,* 257–288.

Greene, F. (1979). Radio reading. In C. Pennock (Ed.), *Reading comprehension at four linguistic levels,* pp. 104–107. Newark, DE: International Reading Association.

Griffith, L., & Rasinski, T. V. (2002, November). *Readers theater promotes fluency and achievement.* Paper presented at the annual meeting of the College Reading Association, Philadelphia, PA.

Gunning, T. (1995). Word building: A strategic approach to the teaching of phonics. *The Reading Teacher, 48,* 484–488.

Harris, T. L., & Hodges, R. E. (Eds.) (1995). *The literacy dictionary: The vocabulary of reading and writing.* Newark, DE: International Reading Association.

Hasbrouck, J. E., Ihnot, C., & Rogers, G. (1999). Read naturally: A strategy to increase oral reading fluency. *Reading Research and Instruction, 39,* 27–38.

Hasbrouck, J. E., & Tindal, G. (1992). Curriculum-based oral reading fluency norms for students in grades 2 through 5. *Teaching Exceptional Children, 24,* 41–44.

Heckelman, R. G. (1969). A neurological impress method of reading instruction. *Academic Therapy, 4,* 277–282.

Herman, P. A. (1985). The effect of repeated readings on reading rate, speech pauses, and word recognition accuracy. *Reading Research Quarterly, 20,* 553–564.

Hecker, L., Burns, L., Elkind, J., Elkind, K., & Katz, L. (2002). Benefits of assistive reading software for students with attention disorders. *Annals of Dyslexia, 52,* 243–272.

Hoffman, J. V. (1991). Teacher and school effects in learning to read. In R. Barr, M. Kamil, P. Mosenthal, & P. D. Pearson (Eds.), *Handbook of reading research,* Vol. II, pp. 911–950. White Plains, NY: Longman.

Hoffman, J. V., & Clements, R. (1984). Reading miscues and teacher verbal feedback. *Elementary School Journal, 84,* 423–440.

Hoffman, J. V., O'Neal, S., Kastler, L., Clements, R., Segel, K., & Nash, M. F. (1984). Guided oral reading and miscue focused verbal feedback in second-grade classrooms. *Reading Research Quarterly, 19*(3), 367–384.

Hoffman, J. V., Roser, N. L., Salas, R., Patterson, E., & Pennington, J. (2001). Text leveling and "little books" in first-grade reading. *Journal of Literacy Research, 33*(3), 507–528.

Hoffman, J. V., & Segel, K. (1983, May). Oral Reading Instruction: A Century of Controversy (1880–1980). Paper presented at the annual meeting of the International Reading Association, Anaheim, CA. (ERIC Document Reproduction Service No. ED239237)

Hollingsworth, P. M. (1978). An experimental approach to the impress method of teaching reading. *The Reading Teacher, 31,* 624–626.

Hoskisson, K. (1975). The many facets of assisted reading. *Elementary English, 52,* 312–315.

Hoskisson, K. (1975). Successive approximation and beginning reading. *Elementary School Journal, 75* (7), 442–451.

Hyatt, A. V. (1943). *The place of oral reading in the school program: Its history and development from 1880–1941.* New York: Teachers College Press.

Invernizzi, M., Juel, C., & Rosemary, C. (1996). A community volunteer tutorial that works. *The Reading Teacher, 50*(4), 304–311.

Invernizzi, M., Rosemary, C., Juel, C., & Richards, H. (1997). At-risk readers and community volunteers: A three-year perspective. *Scientific Studies of Reading, 1*(3), 277–300.

Jackson, J. B., Paratore, J. R., Chard, D. J., & Garnick, S. (1999). An early intervention supporting the literacy learning of children experiencing substantial difficulty. *Learning Disabilities: Research and Practice, 14*(4), 254–267.

Johns, J., & Berglund, R. (2002). *Fluency: Questions, Answers, Evidence-Based Strategies.* Dubuque, IA: Kendall Hunt.

Kame'enui, E. J., & Simmons, D. C. (Ed.) (2001). The role of fluency in reading competence, assessment, and instruction: Fluency at the intersection of accuracy and speed [Special issue]. *Scientific Studies of Reading, 5*(3).

Keillor, G. (2004). For the week of October 18, 2004. *The writer's almanac.* Retrieved April 22, 2007, from http://writersalmanac.publicradio.org/programs/2004/10/18/index.html.

Knapp, N. F., & Winsor, A. P. (1998). A reading apprenticeship for delayed primary readers. *Reading Research and Instruction, 38,* 13–29.

Koskinen, P. S., Blum, I. H., Bisson, S. A., Phillips, S. M., Creamer, T. S., & Baker, T. K. (1999). Shared reading, books, and audiotapes: Supporting diverse students in school and at home. *The Reading Teacher, 52,* 430–444.

Koskinen, P. S., Blum, I. H., Bisson, S. A., Phillips, S. M., Creamer, T. S., & Baker, T. K. (2000). Book access, shared reading, and audio models: The effects of supporting the literacy learning of linguistically diverse students in home and school. *Journal of Educational Psychology, 92*(1), 23–36.

Marston, D. (1989). A curriculum-based measurement approach to assessing academic performance: What it is and why do it. In M. R. Shinn (Ed.), *Curriculum-based measurement: Assessing special children,* pp. 18–78. New York: Guilford.

Martinez, M., & Roser, N. (1985). Read it again: The value of repeated readings during storytime. *The Reading Teacher, 38,* 782–786.

Mathes, P. G., Torgesen, J. K., & Allor, J. H. (2001). The effects of peer-assisted literacy strategies for first-grade readers with and without additional computer-assisted instruction in phonological awareness. *American Educational Research Journal, 38,* 371–410.

Mayer, R. E. (1983). Can you repeat that? Qualitative effects of repetition and advance organizers from science prose. *Journal of Educational Psychology, 75,* 40–49.

Mcgraw, L. K. (2000). Parent tutoring in repeated reading: Effects of procedural adherence on fluency, maintenance, and intervention acceptability. *Dissertation Abstracts International, 60*(7-A), 2372.

Mercer, C. C., Campbell, K. U., Miller, M. D., Mercer, K. D., & Lane, H. B. (2000). Effects of a reading fluency intervention for middle schoolers with specific learning disabilities. *Learning Disabilities: Research and Practice, 15*(4), 179–189.

Meyer, M. S., & Felton, R. H. (1999). Repeated reading to enhance fluency: Old approaches and new directions. *Annals of Dyslexia, 49,* 283–306.

Millin, S. K., & Rinehart, S. D. (1999). Some of the benefits of readers theater participation for second-grade Title I readers. *Reading Research and Instruction, 39,* 71–88.

Morgan, R., & Lyon, E. (1979). Paired reading—A preliminary report on a technique for parental tuition of reading-retarded children. *Journal of Child Psychology and Psychiatry, 20,* 151–160.

Morgan, A., Wilcox, B. R., & Eldredge, J. L. (2000). Effect of difficulty levels on second-grade delayed readers using dyad reading. *Journal of Educational Research, 94,* 113–119.

Moore, R. A., & Aspegren, C. M. (2001). Reflective conversations between two learners: Retrospective miscue analysis. *Journal of Adolescent & Adult Literacy, 44,* 492–503.

Morris, D. (1995). *Early steps: An early intervention program.* Bloomington, IN: ERIC Clearinghouse on Reading, English, and Communication. (ERIC Document Reproduction Service No. ED388956)

Morris, D., & Nelson, L. (1992). Supported oral reading with low achieving second graders. *Reading Research and Instruction, 32,* 49–63.

Morris, D., Shaw, B., & Perney, J. (1990). Helping low readers in grades 2 and 3: An after-school volunteer tutoring program. *Elementary School Journal, 91,* 133–150.

Morris, D., Tyner, B., & Perney, J. (2000). Early steps: Replicating the effects of a first-grade reading intervention program. *Journal of Educational Psychology, 92*(4), 681–693.

Myers, C. A. (1978). Reviewing the literature on Fernald's technique of remedial reading. *The Reading Teacher, 31,* 614–619.

Neill, K. (1980). Turn kids on with repeated reading. *Teaching Exceptional Children, 12,* 63–64.

Opitz, M. F., & Rasinski, T. V. (1998). *Good-bye Round Robin: 25 Effective Oral Reading Strategies.* Portsmouth, NH: Heinemann.

O'Shea, L. J., & Sindelar, P. T. (1983). The effects of segmenting written discourse on the reading comprehension of low- and high-performance readers. *Reading Research Quarterly, 18,* 458–465.

Padak, N., & Rasinski, T. (2005). *Fast Start for Early Readers: A Research-Based, Send-Home Literacy Program.* New York: Scholastic.

Perfect, K. A. (1999). Rhyme and reason: Poetry for the heart and head. *The Reading Teacher, 52,* 728–737.

Person, M. (1990). Say it right! *The Reading Teacher, 43,* 428–429.

Pinnell, G. S., & Fountas, I. C. (1996). *Guided reading: Good first teaching for all children.* Portsmouth, NH: Heinemann.

Pinnell, G. S., Pikulski, J. J., Wixson, K. K., Campbell, J. R., Gough, P. B., & Beatty, A. S. (1995). Listening to children read aloud. Washington, D.C.: U.S. Department of Education, Office of Educational Research and Improvement.

Pluck, M. (1995). Rainbow Reading Programme: Using Taped Stories. *Reading Forum, 1,* 25–29.

Postlethwaite, T. N., & Ross, K. N. (1992). *Effective Schools in Reading: Implications for Policy Planner.* The Hague: International Association for the Evaluation of Educational Achievement.

Prescott, J. O. (2003). The power of reader's theater. *Instructor, 112*(5), 22–26+.

Rasinski, T. V. (1985). A study of factors involved in reader-text interactions that contribute to fluency in reading. Unpublished doctoral dissertation. Columbus, OH: The Ohio State University.

Rasinski, T. V. (1989). Fluency for everyone: Incorporating fluency in the classroom. *The Reading Teacher, 42,* 690–693.

Rasinski, T. V. (1990). *The effects of cued phrase boundaries in texts.* Bloomington, IN: ERIC Clearinghouse on Reading and Communication Skills (ED 313 689).

Rasinski, T. V. (1990). Effects of repeated reading ad listening-while-reading on reading fluency. *Journal of Educational Research, 83,* 147–150.

Rasinski, T. V. (1992). Investigating measures of reading fluency. *Educational Research Quarterly.*

Rasinski, T. V. (1995). Fast Start: A parental involvement reading program for primary grade students. In W. Linek & E. Sturtevant (Eds.), *Generations of literacy. Seventeenth Yearbook of the College Reading Association,* pp. 301–312. Harrisonburg, VA: College Reading Association.

Rasinski, T. V. (2000). Speed does matter in reading. *The Reading Teacher, 54,* 146–151.

Rasinski, T. V. (2003). *The fluent reader: Oral reading strategies for building word recognition, fluency, and comprehension.* New York: Scholastic.

Rasinski, T. V. (2004). *Assessing reading fluency.* Honolulu: Pacific Resources for Education and Learning. Available at www.prel.org.

Rasinski, T. V. (2006). Reading fluency instruction: Moving beyond accuracy, automaticity, and prosody. *The Reading Teacher, 59,* 704–706.

Rasinski, T. V. (In press). Teaching reading fluency artfully: A professional and personal journey. In R. Fink & S. J. Samuels (Eds.), *Inspiring reading success: Interest and motivation in an age of high-stakes testing.* Newark, DE: International Reading Association.

Rasinski, T., Blachowicz, C., & Lems, K. (2006). *Fluency instruction: Research-based best practices.* New York: Guilford.

Rasinski, T. V., & Fredericks, A. D. (1991). The Akron paired reading project. *The Reading Teacher, 44,* 514–515.

Rasinski, T. V., & Padak, N. (2000). *Effective Reading Strategies: Teaching children who find reading difficult* (2nd ed.). Columbus, OH: Merrill/Prentice Hall.

Rasinski, T. V., & Padak, N. (2004). *Effective reading strategies: Teaching children who find reading difficult* (3rd ed.). Columbus, OH: Merrill/Prentice Hall.

Rasinski, T. V., & Padak, N. D. (2001). *From phonics to fluency: Effective teaching of decoding and reading fluency in the elementary school.* New York: Longman.

Rasinski, T. V., & Padak, N. (2005). *Three-minute reading assessments: Word recognition, fluency, and comprehesnion for grades 1–4.* New York: Scholastic.

Rasinski, T. V., & Padak, N. (2005). *Three-minute reading assessments: Word recognition, fluency, and comprehension for grades 5–8.* New York: Scholastic.

Rasinski, T. V., & Padak, N. D. (2005). Fluency beyond the primary grades: Helping adolescent readers. *Voices from the Middle, 13,* 34–41.

Rasinski, T., Padak, N., McKeon, C., Krug,-Wilfong, L., Friedauer, J., & Heim, P. (2005). Is reading fluency a key for successful high school reading? *Journal of Adolescent and Adult Literacy, 49,* 22–27.

Rasinski, T., & Stevenson, B. (2005). The effects of fast start reading, a fluency based home involvement reading program, on the reading achievement of beginning readers. *Reading Psychology: An International Quarterly, 26,* 109–125.

Rasinski, T. V., & Zutell, J. B. (1996). Is fluency yet a goal of the reading curriculum? In E. G. Sturtevant & W. M. Linek (Eds.), *Growing literacy: 18th Yearbook of the College Reading Association,* pp. 237–246. Harrisonburg, VA: College Reading Association.

Reitsma, P. (1988). Reading practice for beginners: Effects of guided reading, reading-while-listening, and independent reading with computer-based speech. *Reading Research Quarterly, 23,* 219–235.

Rinehart, S. D. (1999). "Don't think for a minute that I'm getting up there": Opportunities for reader's theater in a tutorial for children with reading problems. *Reading Psychology: An International Quarterly, 20,* 71–89.

Rosenblatt, L. (1978). The reader, the text, and the poem: *The transactional theory of literary work.* Carbondale, IL: Southern Illinois University Press.

Samuels, S. J. (1979). The method of repeated readings. *The Reading Teacher, 32,* 403–408. Also in *The Reading Teacher* (1997, February), pages 376+.

Santa, C. M., & Hoien, T. (1999). An assessment of Early Steps: A program for early intervention of reading problems. *Reading Research Quarterly, 34*(1), 54–79.

Schreiber, P. A. (1980). On the acquisition of reading fluency. *Journal of Reading Behavior, 12,* 177–186.

Schreiber, P. A. (1987). Prosody and structure in children's syntactic processing. In R. Horowitz & S. J. Samuels (Eds.), *Comprehending oral and written language,* pp. 243–270. New York: Academic Press.

Schreiber, P. A. (1991). Understanding prosody's role in reading acquisition. *Theory into Practice, 30,* 158–164.

Schreiber, P. A., & Read, C. (1980). Children's use of phonetic cues in spelling, parsing, and—maybe—reading. *Bulletin of the Orton Society, 30,* 209–224.

Searfoss, L. (1975). Radio Reading. *The Reading Teacher, 29,* 295–296.

Semonick, M. A. (2001). T*he effects of paired repeated reading on second graders oral reading and on-task behavior. Dissertation Abstracts International, 62* (3-1A), 914.

Sindelar, P. T., Monda, L. E., & O'Shea, L. J. (1990). Effects of repeated readings on instructional- and mastery-level readers. *Journal of Educational Research, 83,* 220–226.

Smith, J., & Elley, W. (1997). *How children learn to read: Insights from the New Zealand experience.* Katonah, NY: Richard C. Owen.

Snow, C. E., Burns, M. S., & Griffin, P. (1998). *Preventing reading difficulties in young children.* Washington, D.C.: National Academy Press.

Stahl, S. A. (1992). Saying the "p" word: Nine guidelines for exemplary phonics instruction. *The Reading Teacher, 45,* 618–625.

Stahl, S., & Heubach, K. (2005). Fluency-oriented reading instruction. *Journal of Literacy Research, 37,* 25–60.

Stahl, S. A., Heubach, K., & Cramond, B. (1997). *Fluency-oriented reading instruction,* Reading research report no. 79. Athens, GA, and College Park, MD: National Reading Research Center.

Stallings, J. (1980). Allocated academic learning time revisited, or beyond time on task. *Educational Researcher, 9,* 11–16.

Stanovich, K. E. (1980). Toward an interactive-compensatory model of individual differences in the development of reading fluency. *Reading Research Quarterly, 16,* 32–71.

Stevenson, B. (2002). *The efficacy of the Fast Start parent tutoring program in the development of reading skills of first-grade students.* Unpublished doctoral dissertation, The Ohio State University, Columbus.

Strecker, S., Roser, N., & Martinez, N. (1998). Toward an understanding of oral reading fluency. In T. Shanahan & F. Rodriguez-Brown (Eds.), *Forty-seventh Yearbook of the National Reading Conference,* pp. 295–310. Chicago: National Reading Conference.

Topping, K. (1987). Paired reading: A powerful technique for parent use. *The Reading Teacher, 40,* 604–614.

Topping, K. (1987). Peer tutored paired reading: Outcome data from ten projects. *Educational Psychology, 7,* 133–145.

Topping, K. (1989). Peer tutoring and paired reading. Combining two powerful techniques. *The Reading Teacher, 42,* 488–494.

Topping, K. (1995). *Paired reading, spelling, and writing.* New York: Cassell.

Tyler, B. J., & Chard, D. (2000). Using readers theater to foster fluency in struggling readers: A twist on the repeated reading strategy. *Reading and Writing Quarterly, 16,* 163–168.

Wheldall, K. (2000). Does Rainbow repeated reading add value to an intensive literacy intervention program for low-progress readers? An experimental evaluation. *Educational Review, 52*(1), 29–36.

Wilkinson, I., Wardrop, J. L., & Anderson, R. C. (1988). Silent reading reconsidered: Reinterpreting reading instruction and its effects. *American Educational Research Journal, 25,* 127–144.

Willingham, D. (2007). The usefulness of brief instruction in reading comprehension strategies. *American Educator, 30,* 39–50.

Worthy, J., & Prater, K. (2002). "I thought about it all night": Readers Theater for reading fluency and motivation. *The Reading Teacher, 56,* 294–297.

Zutell, J., & Rasinski, T. V. (1991). Training teachers to attend to their students' oral reading fluency in. *Theory to Practice, 30,* 211–217.